HowExpert Guide to Disc Golf

The Ultimate Handbook for Playing, Competing, and Mastering Disc Golf – From Beginner to Pro

HowExpert

For more tips related to this topic, visit HowExpert.com/discgolf.

Recommended Resources

- HowExpert.com – How To Guides on All Topics from A to Z.
- HowExpert.com/free – Free HowExpert Email Newsletter.
- HowExpert.com/books – HowExpert Books
- HowExpert.com/courses – HowExpert Courses
- HowExpert.com/clothing – HowExpert Clothing
- HowExpert.com/membership – HowExpert Membership Site
- HowExpert.com/affiliates – HowExpert Affiliate Program
- HowExpert.com/jobs – HowExpert Jobs
- HowExpert.com/writers – Write About Your #1 Passion/Knowledge/Expertise & Become a HowExpert Author.
- HowExpert.com/resources – Additional HowExpert Recommended Resources
- YouTube.com/HowExpert – Subscribe to HowExpert YouTube.
- Instagram.com/HowExpert – Follow HowExpert on Instagram.
- Facebook.com/HowExpert – Follow HowExpert on Facebook.
- TikTok.com/@HowExpert – Follow HowExpert on TikTok.

Publisher's Foreword

Dear HowExpert Reader,

HowExpert publishes quick 'how to' guides on all topics from A to Z.

Our mission is to make a positive impact in the world for all topics from A to Z…one HowExpert book at a time!

We are dedicated to creating quick, easy-to-read 'how to' guides that are structured, comprehensive, and approachable, empowering our readers to effortlessly explore and learn about their passions and interests in a meaningful and enjoyable way.

We hope our HowExpert books bring you immense value and make a positive impact on your life. Every reader, including you, plays a vital role in helping us fulfill our mission of making a positive difference in the world across all areas of interest from A to Z.

If you enjoyed one of our HowExpert guides, we would greatly appreciate it if you could take a moment to share your feedback on the platform where you discovered this book.

Thank you, and I wish you success and happiness in all aspects of your life.

To your success,

BJ Min
Founder & Publisher of HowExpert
HowExpert.com
John 14:6

Table of Contents

Book Overview

HowExpert Guide to Disc Golf: The Ultimate Handbook for Playing, Competing, and Mastering Disc Golf – From Beginner to Pro

If you want to throw farther, improve accuracy, and lower your scores in disc golf, *HowExpert Guide to Disc Golf* is your complete resource for learning and mastering the game. Whether you are stepping onto the course for the first time, refining your form, or preparing for competitive tournaments, this book will help you develop consistency, make smarter shot selections, and improve every aspect of your game.

Disc golf is more than just throwing a disc — it's about precision, strategy, and confidence. Knowing how to control your shots, navigate different course layouts, and adapt to various conditions can take your performance to the next level. This book provides a step-by-step approach, breaking down the fundamentals and advanced techniques into clear, actionable lessons so you can see real improvement in your game.

Inside, you'll discover:

- **Chapter 1 – Understanding the Game**: Learn the fundamentals, including rules, scoring, and the unique spirit of fair play in disc golf.

- **Chapter 2 – Essential Disc Golf Gear**: Choose the right discs, understand flight ratings, and discover must-have accessories for better performance.

- **Chapter 3 – Course Layout & Strategy**: Break down the elements of a disc golf course, analyze different terrains, and develop a game plan for any situation.

- **Chapter 4 – The Fundamentals of Throwing**: Master key throwing techniques, including backhand, forehand (flick), overhand, and advanced shot types.

- **Chapter 5 – Perfecting Your Putting Game**: Build a consistent putting stroke, develop a pre-putt routine, and improve accuracy inside and outside the circle.

- **Chapter 6 – Disc Golf Strategy & Course Management**: Learn shot selection, risk vs. reward decision-making, and how to adjust to changing conditions.

- **Chapter 7 – Training, Fitness & Disc Golf Performance**: Strengthen your body for power and endurance, increase flexibility, and prevent injuries.

- **Chapter 8 – Tournaments & Competitive Play**: Prepare for PDGA events, learn tournament etiquette, and manage nerves in high-pressure situations.

- **Chapter 9 – The Mental Game of Disc Golf**: Stay focused, bounce back from bad throws, and develop the confidence needed to play your best.

- **Chapter 10 – Growing the Sport & Getting Involved**: Introduce new players to the game, run leagues and tournaments, and contribute to the disc golf community.

- **Chapter 11 – Creative & Alternative Ways to Play**: Explore trick shots, glow disc golf, safari layouts, and unique ways to have fun on the course.

- **Conclusion**: Keep learning, refining your skills, and enjoying disc golf for a lifetime.

- **Appendices**: Access a glossary of key disc golf terms, recommended gear and brands, a list of must-play courses, and valuable training resources.

Whether you play casually, are working toward personal goals, or are training for serious competition, *HowExpert Guide to Disc Golf* provides the knowledge and techniques to take your game to the next level. With simple techniques, practical strategies, and real-world insights, this book will help you throw with more power, putt with more confidence, and enjoy disc golf even more.

Grab your discs, step up to the tee, and start improving — one throw at a time.

HowExpert publishes how to guides on all topics from A to Z. Visit HowExpert.com to learn more.

Introduction

Disc golf has grown from a simple backyard pastime into a dynamic, competitive sport played by thousands of athletes worldwide. *HowExpert Guide to Disc Golf* is your go-to resource for learning, improving, and mastering the game—whether you're a casual player, an aspiring competitor, or someone looking for a fun and engaging outdoor activity. This guide breaks down every essential aspect of disc golf, from the fundamentals to advanced techniques, to help you develop your skills, make smarter game decisions, and enjoy the sport to its fullest.

From backyard games to professional tournaments—disc golf offers a journey for every player!

I. The Rise of Disc Golf: From Backyard Game to Competitive Sport

Disc golf traces its roots back to the 1970s, when a small group of enthusiasts began throwing discs at makeshift targets in parks and open fields. Over the years, the sport has evolved into a structured and competitive game, complete with standardized rules, professional tournaments, and thousands of courses worldwide. The Professional

Disc Golf Association (PDGA) was established to bring organization and legitimacy to the sport, paving the way for its rapid growth.

Today, disc golf attracts players of all ages and skill levels, from casual throwers enjoying a round with friends to elite athletes competing in national and international championships. The sport's accessibility, low cost, and easy learning curve have made it one of the fastest-growing outdoor activities in the world. With new courses being designed regularly and technology improving disc performance, disc golf is more exciting and competitive than ever before.

II. Why Disc Golf? The Perfect Sport for All Ages & Skill Levels

One of the biggest reasons disc golf has exploded in popularity is that it is easy to start but challenging to master. Unlike traditional golf, which requires expensive equipment, club memberships, and extensive practice, disc golf allows players to get started with just a few discs and a local course. The sport is also incredibly inclusive— people of all ages, athletic abilities, and backgrounds can enjoy it.

Disc golf offers a unique blend of strategy, skill, and outdoor adventure. It improves hand-eye coordination, builds endurance, and encourages creative problem-solving as players navigate diverse course layouts and challenging terrain. Whether you're looking for a casual weekend activity or a serious competitive sport, disc golf delivers an engaging experience for everyone.

III. Who This Book Is For: Casual Players, Competitive Athletes & Enthusiasts

HowExpert Guide to Disc Golf is designed for players of all skill levels, offering valuable insights no matter where you are in your disc golf journey.

- Beginners will find step-by-step guidance on throwing techniques, choosing discs, understanding the rules, and developing fundamental skills.

- Intermediate players will learn how to refine their form, improve accuracy, build a stronger mental game, and develop smart strategies for different courses.

- Advanced players and competitors will discover advanced shot techniques, expert-level strategy, fitness training for disc golf, and how to prepare for high-level tournaments.

- Coaches, parents, and disc golf enthusiasts will gain valuable insights into teaching, growing the sport, and getting involved in the disc golf community.

Whether you're picking up a disc for the first time or looking to take your skills to the next level, this book will help you improve, compete, and enjoy disc golf more than ever.

IV. How to Use This Guide: Learning, Improving & Dominating the Game

This book is structured to take you through every stage of disc golf development, from learning the basics to mastering advanced techniques. Each chapter is packed with practical advice, strategies, and real-world applications to help you improve your game step by step.

- Part 1 covers the fundamentals of disc golf, including the rules, essential gear, and how to navigate different courses.

- Part 2 focuses on throwing mechanics, putting techniques, and shot selection, ensuring you build a strong foundation.

- Part 3 dives into strategy, course management, mental preparation, and training to refine your game.

- Part 4 explores competitive play, growing the sport, and creative ways to enjoy disc golf beyond traditional rounds.

- The Appendices provide additional resources, including a glossary of terms, recommended gear, and a list of must-play courses.

You can read this book in order or jump to specific chapters depending on what you want to focus on. Whether you're fine-tuning your technique, preparing for a tournament, or looking to deepen your love for the sport, *HowExpert Guide to Disc Golf* is your comprehensive playbook for success on the course.

Part 1: Disc Golf Fundamentals

Before advancing to higher-level strategies or competitions, every disc golfer must develop a solid foundation. This section introduces the essential elements of disc golf, including its rules, scoring, and etiquette, ensuring you play with confidence and sportsmanship. You'll explore the different types of discs—drivers, midranges, and putters—along with must-have accessories and the best footwear for performance. Additionally, we'll cover disc golf course layouts, terrain challenges, and strategic navigation to help you plan your shots effectively. Understanding these fundamentals will allow you to adapt to different courses, improve accuracy, and build consistency. Whether you're a complete beginner or refining your basics, mastering these core principles will set you up for success and enjoyment on the course.

Chapter 1: Understanding the Game

Disc golf is more than just throwing a disc—it's a sport built on skill, strategy, and sportsmanship. To play with confidence, you need a solid grasp of its fundamentals. This chapter covers what disc golf is, how it's played, and the key rules, scoring, and objectives that shape the game. You'll also learn about the sport's emphasis on fair play, etiquette, and respect for fellow players. Whether you're a first-time player or reinforcing your knowledge, this chapter lays the foundation for success on the course, ensuring you understand both the mechanics and the spirit of disc golf.

Every great disc golfer starts with the fundamentals—master the basics and build your game!

1.1 What is Disc Golf? A Breakdown of the Sport

Disc golf is an exciting and rapidly growing sport that combines the precision and strategy of traditional golf with the accessibility and fun of throwing a flying disc. Instead of clubs and balls, players use specialized discs to complete a course made up of metal baskets, aiming to finish each hole in as few throws as possible. Played in parks, forests, and open fields, disc golf is a sport for all ages and skill levels. Whether you're picking up a disc for the first time or competing at a professional level, disc golf offers a rewarding challenge that blends skill, strategy, and outdoor enjoyment.

Disc golf blends strategy, precision, and outdoor adventure into a unique and accessible sport.

A. The Basics of Disc Golf

Disc golf follows a structure similar to traditional golf but replaces clubs and balls with flying discs. The goal is to complete a course by throwing the disc from the tee area to the metal basket in as few strokes as possible. Players must navigate obstacles such as trees, elevation changes, and out-of-bounds areas while aiming for accuracy and control. While the game is easy to learn, mastering different throwing techniques, disc selections, and course strategies takes time and practice.

- **Start at the tee pad** – Each hole begins with a throw from a designated tee pad, where players launch their disc toward the target.

- **Advance toward the basket** – Players throw their next shot from where their previous disc landed, continuing until they complete the hole.

- **Count strokes** – Every throw is counted as a stroke, and the goal is to finish the course with the fewest total strokes.

- **Follow course rules** – Some holes have **mandatories (mandos)** requiring discs to pass a certain side of an obstacle, as well as **out-of-bounds (OB) areas** that result in penalty strokes.

Disc Golf vs. Traditional Golf

Feature	Disc Golf	Traditional Golf
Equipment	Discs (driver, midrange, putter)	Clubs and balls
Target	Metal basket with chains	Hole with a flagstick
Playing surface	Parks, wooded areas, open fields	Grass fairways, bunkers, greens
Cost to play	Often free or low cost	Can be expensive (green fees, memberships)
Skill focus	Throwing technique, disc control	Swing mechanics, ball control

Disc golf is easier to start and much more affordable than traditional golf, making it a popular option for casual and competitive players alike.

B. A Sport for Everyone

Disc golf is one of the most accessible sports, welcoming players of all ages, backgrounds, and skill levels. With minimal equipment requirements and free-to-play courses in many areas, it is an easy sport to pick up and enjoy. The simplicity of the game makes it inviting for beginners, while the depth of strategy and precision keeps advanced players engaged.

- **Affordable** – Many public courses are free, and a beginner disc set costs much less than traditional sports equipment.

- **Easy to Learn** – The basic concept is simple: throw the disc toward the basket. Even beginners can enjoy playing on day one.

- **Great for All Ages** – Kids, adults, and seniors can all play, making it a lifelong sport.

- **No Special Gear Needed** – While players can upgrade their gear over time, a single disc is all that's needed to get started.

- **Can Be Played Solo or With Friends** – Whether you want to challenge yourself or play in a group, disc golf fits any setting.

Disc golf courses continue to expand worldwide, offering an accessible and engaging outdoor activity for individuals and communities alike.

C. The Evolution and Growth of Disc Golf

Although disc golf has roots tracing back to informal frisbee-throwing games, its official rise as a structured sport began in the 1970s. The sport has since evolved into a global phenomenon with professional tours, sponsorships, and televised events.

- **1960s** – Early forms of disc golf were played in parks and open areas using trees and objects as targets.

- **1975** – Ed Headrick, known as the "Father of Disc Golf," created the first chain basket target, revolutionizing the sport.

- **1976** – The **Professional Disc Golf Association (PDGA)** was founded, formalizing the rules and structure of the game.

- **1990s-2000s** – Courses expanded worldwide, and the sport grew in popularity through tournaments and local clubs.

- **Present Day** – Disc golf is now a professional sport with thousands of courses, major sponsorships, and a rapidly growing global presence.

With increased media coverage, disc golf is reaching new audiences and becoming one of the fastest-growing sports in the world.

D. More Than Just a Game

For many players, disc golf is more than just a casual pastime—it fosters personal growth, social interaction, and a deep connection with nature. The game offers mental and physical benefits while encouraging outdoor activity and strategic thinking.

- **Improves Physical Health** – Walking courses, throwing discs, and navigating terrain provide a great workout.

- **Enhances Mental Focus** – Reading the course, planning shots, and staying composed under pressure sharpen concentration and problem-solving skills.

- **Promotes Social Interaction** – Many players meet new people and build friendships through leagues, tournaments, and casual rounds.

- **Encourages Outdoor Activity** – Playing in parks and natural settings provides fresh air, relaxation, and a break from screen time.

- **Builds Confidence** – Achieving personal milestones and improving skills over time gives players a sense of accomplishment.

Disc golf instills values like patience, perseverance, and sportsmanship, making it a sport that fosters both personal and competitive growth.

E. Key Takeaways

Disc golf is an accessible and fast-growing sport that blends skill, strategy, and outdoor enjoyment. Whether you are playing for fun or competing at a high level, disc golf offers a unique experience that challenges both physical and mental abilities.

- **Disc golf basics** – Players throw discs toward a metal basket, completing each hole in the fewest throws possible. The game follows a similar structure to traditional golf but is played in parks, forests, and open fields.

- **Accessible for all** – With free courses, affordable gear, and an easy learning curve, disc golf is open to players of all ages and skill levels.

- **Rapid growth** – Since the 1970s, disc golf has expanded globally, with professional tours, sponsorships, and increasing media exposure.

- **More than just a game** – The sport offers physical, mental, and social benefits, fostering personal development and lifelong learning.

As disc golf continues to grow worldwide, more people are discovering the joy and challenge of the sport. Now that you understand the basics of what disc golf is, the next section explores how to play the game, including rules, objectives, and scoring systems.

1.2 How to Play: Rules, Objectives & Scoring System

Disc golf is an exciting sport with simple yet strategic gameplay that appeals to both beginners and experienced players. While the core objective is easy to understand—throw a disc into a metal basket in the fewest throws possible—mastering the game requires knowledge of its rules, scoring system, and strategic elements. This section provides a complete breakdown of how to play disc golf, covering everything from basic gameplay to official tournament rules. Whether you're a casual player looking to enjoy a round at your local course or aiming to compete in organized events, understanding the fundamentals of disc golf will set you up for success.

Master the rules and scoring system to sharpen your disc golf strategy.

A. The Objective of the Game

The goal of disc golf is to complete a course in the fewest possible throws. Each hole begins at a tee pad and ends at a metal basket, with players advancing their disc from the spot where their previous throw landed. Players compete to achieve the lowest total strokes by navigating a course that features various terrain, obstacles, and distances. While casual rounds focus on self-improvement and practice, competitive play follows a structured format where players take turns throwing based on distance from the basket.

- **Par 3** – The most common hole type, requiring three throws for an average player.

- **Par 4** – A longer hole that often requires strategic placement of shots.

- **Par 5** – The longest and most challenging holes, typically requiring multiple controlled throws before attempting to putt.

Each hole presents unique challenges, including trees, elevation changes, and water hazards. Players must develop strategic shot selection, adjusting their approach based on the course layout.

B. The Rules of Play

Disc golf follows structured rules that ensure fair competition and consistency. Players must adhere to regulations regarding throwing order, disc placement, and penalties, which are designed to maintain fairness while allowing for strategic decision-making. These rules apply to both casual play and formal tournaments.

- **Throwing Order** – On the first hole, players determine their throwing order randomly or by agreement. After the first throw, the player farthest from the basket always throws next.

- **Throwing from the Lie** – After each throw, players must throw their next shot from the spot where their disc landed. A mini marker can be placed in front of the disc to mark the exact position.

- **Out-of-Bounds (OB) and Hazards** – If a disc lands in a designated OB area (e.g., water, roads, or private property), a penalty stroke is added, and the player must throw from either the previous lie or a designated drop zone.

- **Mandatories (Mandos)** – Some holes have mandatory obstacles, requiring players to throw to a specific side of a tree or pole. Missing a mando results in a penalty stroke.

- **Holing Out** – A hole is completed when the disc comes to rest inside the basket or chains. Discs that land on top of the basket do not count as completed.

While these are the general rules of play, official tournaments follow the standards set by the **Professional Disc Golf Association (PDGA)**, which include more detailed regulations and enforcement guidelines.

C. Scoring System & Terminology

Disc golf scoring follows a stroke-based system where the goal is to complete each hole in as few throws as possible. Players keep track of their total strokes across all holes to determine the final score, with lower scores indicating better performance. Understanding scoring terminology is essential for both casual and competitive play.

- **Birdie (-1)** – Completing a hole one stroke under par (e.g., scoring a 2 on a par 3).

- **Eagle (-2)** – Completing a hole two strokes under par (e.g., scoring a 3 on a par 5).

- **Albatross (-3)** – Completing a hole three strokes under par (a rare achievement).

- **Par (0)** – Completing a hole in the expected number of throws (e.g., 3 on a par 3).

- **Bogey (+1)** – Completing a hole one stroke over par (e.g., scoring a 4 on a par 3).

- **Double Bogey (+2)** – Completing a hole two strokes over par (e.g., scoring a 5 on a par 3).

- **Triple Bogey (+3)** – Completing a hole three strokes over par (e.g., scoring a 6 on a par 3).

Most casual players aim to play at or below par, while advanced players focus on scoring birdies and eagles to stay competitive in tournaments. In tournament play, the player with the lowest total strokes across all holes wins, though some events use match play scoring, where players compete hole-by-hole.

D. Common Game Formats & Variations

Disc golf offers a variety of game formats beyond traditional stroke play, allowing players to experience new challenges and develop different skills. These formats are ideal for both casual rounds and competitive play, offering diverse ways to enjoy the game.

- **Singles Play** – Each player competes individually, aiming for the lowest overall score.

- **Doubles Play** – Two-player teams take turns throwing, with the best throw being chosen for the next shot.

- **Match Play** – Instead of counting total strokes, players compete hole-by-hole, earning a point for each hole they win.

- **Alternate Shot** – In doubles format, players take turns throwing, requiring more teamwork and strategy.

- **Safari Golf** – Players modify the course layout, creating new holes and unique challenges.

- **Speed Golf** – Players complete the course as quickly as possible, combining fast play with accuracy for an endurance-based challenge.

E. Key Takeaways

Mastering the rules and scoring system of disc golf is essential for both casual and competitive players. By understanding the fundamentals, players can improve their performance, make strategic decisions, and fully enjoy the game. Disc golf is not just about throwing a disc—it's about precision, decision-making, and adaptability to various course conditions.

- **Disc golf rules** – Players must complete each hole with the fewest throws while following fair play rules, including OB penalties and mandatory shot directions.

- **Scoring system** – Scores are based on strokes relative to par, with birdies and eagles being positive achievements while bogeys indicate over-par performance.

- **Game variations** – Different formats, such as match play, doubles, and speed golf, offer unique ways to enjoy the sport.

Whether playing casually with friends or competing in professional tournaments, having a solid grasp of the rules, scoring, and variations enhances the overall disc golf experience. The next section will explore the spirit of the game, including etiquette, fair play, and sportsmanship.

1.3 The Spirit of the Game: Etiquette, Fair Play & Sportsmanship

Disc golf is more than just throwing discs and keeping score—it is a sport built on respect, integrity, and camaraderie. The spirit of the game emphasizes fair play, personal responsibility, and consideration for fellow players, the course, and the environment. While official rules ensure structure and fairness, good etiquette and sportsmanship define the culture of disc golf, making it an enjoyable experience for everyone. Whether playing casually or competing at the highest level, understanding and embracing the spirit of the game is essential for every disc golfer.

Disc golf isn't just about competition—it's about respect, integrity, and community.

A. The Importance of Etiquette in Disc Golf

Etiquette in disc golf refers to the unspoken rules and respectful behaviors that keep the game enjoyable, safe, and fair for all players. Unlike many sports with referees or officials overseeing gameplay, disc golf relies heavily on self-regulation and honesty, making etiquette a crucial part of the game's integrity. By following proper etiquette, players create a positive and welcoming atmosphere on the course, ensuring that everyone has an enjoyable experience.

- **Respect turn order** – Always allow the player farthest from the basket to throw first and avoid distracting others during their shots.

- **Stay quiet during throws** – Conversations, unnecessary movement, and sudden noises can disrupt a player's focus.

- **Give players space** – Stand behind or to the side of a player as they throw to avoid being in their line of sight.

- **Be ready to throw** – Keep the game moving by preparing for your turn while others are throwing, but without causing distractions.

- **Avoid damaging the course** – Do not break branches, litter, or leave behind any trash. Many courses are maintained by volunteers who work hard to keep them in good shape.

- **Let faster groups play through** – If your group is playing slowly and a faster group is behind you, allow them to pass to maintain course flow.

- **Help find lost discs** – If another player loses a disc, offer assistance in searching for it to keep the game fair and enjoyable.

B. Fair Play & Integrity

One of the defining aspects of disc golf is that players are responsible for enforcing rules and calling penalties on themselves. Honesty and integrity are fundamental to the game, and players are expected to follow the rules even when no one is watching. Maintaining fair play ensures that all players compete on an even playing field, upholding the integrity of the sport and fostering mutual respect among competitors.

- **Call penalties fairly** – If a rule is broken (such as stepping past the lie or throwing from an illegal position), acknowledge the mistake and apply the correct penalty.

- **Respect mando and OB calls** – If a shot misses a mandatory route or lands out of bounds, accept the penalty stroke without argument.

- **Do not take extra throws** – Avoid throwing extra shots during a round unless practicing in an allowed area.

- **Resolve disputes calmly** – If a rules question arises, discuss it with your group and refer to the PDGA rulebook if necessary.

C. Sportsmanship & Positive Attitude

Good sportsmanship goes beyond just following the rules—it's about respecting your competitors, handling both success and failure gracefully, and fostering a positive playing environment. Encouraging and supporting fellow players, regardless of skill level, strengthens the disc golf community and enhances the enjoyment of the game for everyone.

- **Encourage others** – Congratulate great shots from your fellow players, regardless of whether they are on your card or competing against you.

- **Keep a positive attitude** – Disc golf is meant to be fun, so avoid excessive complaining about bad shots, weather conditions, or unlucky breaks.

- **Respect all skill levels** – Whether playing with beginners or professionals, treat everyone with the same level of respect and encouragement.

- **Accept bad throws gracefully** – Every player has off days. Learn from mistakes instead of letting frustration affect your game or others' enjoyment.

- **Acknowledge opponents** – At the end of a round, thank your playing partners for the game, regardless of the outcome.

D. Respect for the Course & the Environment

Many disc golf courses are located in public parks, forests, and natural areas, making it essential for players to respect the environment and help preserve course conditions. Responsible play ensures that courses remain open, clean, and enjoyable for future players. By taking care of the course, players contribute to the long-term sustainability of the sport and demonstrate appreciation for the spaces that allow disc golf to thrive.

- **Pack out trash** – Always clean up after yourself, even if trash bins are available. Leave the course cleaner than you found it.

- **Follow course rules** – Some courses have specific rules regarding paths, restricted areas, or park hours—respect these guidelines.

- **Avoid damaging nature** – Do not break branches, pull up grass, or alter the course to improve a shot.

- **Return lost discs** – If you find a disc with contact information, make an effort to return it to its owner.

- **Respect other park users** – Many disc golf courses share space with walkers, joggers, and picnickers. Always yield the right of way and ensure safety for everyone.

E. Key Takeaways

The spirit of disc golf is built on values that promote respect, honesty, and fair competition. Practicing good etiquette, maintaining integrity, and demonstrating sportsmanship all contribute to a positive and rewarding playing experience.

- **Etiquette matters** – Players should respect turn order, stay quiet during throws, and keep the course clean to ensure a smooth and enjoyable game.

- **Fair play is essential** – Self-enforcement of rules and penalties ensures that every player competes with integrity and mutual respect.

- **Sportsmanship strengthens the game** – Encouraging fellow players, maintaining a positive attitude, and handling both success and failure with grace create a welcoming atmosphere.

- **Course preservation is key** – Keeping courses clean, respecting natural elements, and following park rules ensure that disc golf remains accessible and enjoyable for years to come.

By embracing these principles, disc golfers contribute to a positive playing experience for themselves and others. The next section will explore the essential disc golf gear needed to play at your best.

Chapter 1 Review: Understanding the Game

Chapter 1 establishes the core fundamentals of disc golf, explaining what the sport is, how it is played, and the essential principles of fair play and sportsmanship. It provides a clear breakdown of the game's objectives, rules, and scoring system while emphasizing the importance of etiquette, integrity, and respect for both players and the course. Whether you're new to disc golf or refining your understanding, this chapter lays the foundation for a confident and enjoyable playing experience.

1.1 What is Disc Golf? A Breakdown of the Sport

- **A blend of skill and strategy** – Disc golf merges elements of traditional golf with the unique challenge of precision disc throwing.

- **Played in diverse environments** – Courses range from wooded trails to open fields, each offering distinct challenges.

- **Simple yet competitive** – The goal is to complete each hole in as few throws as possible, with courses typically featuring 9 or 18 holes.

- **A fast-growing sport** – What began as a casual pastime has evolved into a global phenomenon with professional tours and thousands of courses worldwide.

- **Accessible to all** – With minimal equipment costs and no required memberships, disc golf welcomes players of all ages and skill levels.

1.2 How to Play: Rules, Objectives & Scoring System

- **The basic objective** – Players throw a disc from the tee pad toward a metal basket, aiming for the lowest number of throws.

- **Turn-based gameplay** – Players take turns throwing, advancing from where their disc lands until they complete the hole.

- **Scoring system** – Players earn scores based on strokes relative to par, with common terms including birdie (-1), par (0), and bogey (+1).

- **Game variations** – While stroke play is the standard, formats like match play, doubles, and safari golf add unique challenges.

- **Strategy makes a difference** – Smart shot selection, effective course management, and adaptability are key to lowering scores.

1.3 The Spirit of the Game: Etiquette, Fair Play & Sportsmanship

- **Self-regulated gameplay** – Players are responsible for following the rules, enforcing penalties, and maintaining fair play.

- **Respect for fellow players** – Staying quiet during throws, observing turn order, and keeping pace ensures an enjoyable round.

- **Honesty is key** – Disc golfers are expected to uphold integrity in scoring, penalty calls, and overall conduct.

- **Sportsmanship matters** – Encouraging others, maintaining composure, and handling victories and setbacks with grace enhances the playing experience.

- **Respect for the environment** – Preserving courses by avoiding damage, disposing of trash properly, and following park regulations supports the sport's future.

Chapter 1 provides a comprehensive introduction to disc golf, ensuring players step onto the course with a strong understanding of the game. The next chapter dives into essential disc golf gear, including the different types of discs, key accessories, and how to choose the right equipment for your playing style.

Chapter 2: Essential Disc Golf Gear

The right gear enhances performance, comfort, and consistency on the course. While disc golf requires only a few discs, selecting the right ones improves control and overall play. This chapter explores the three main disc types—drivers, midranges, and putters—each suited for different shots. Understanding plastic types, weights, and flight ratings helps build a well-rounded selection. Beyond discs, accessories like bags, mini markers, and towels add convenience. Proper footwear and apparel provide stability, traction, and comfort on varied terrain. By the end of this chapter, you'll know how to choose the best discs, gear, and apparel to match your needs and elevate your game.

The right gear can elevate your game—choose wisely and play with confidence.

2.1 Disc Types: Drivers, Midranges & Putters Explained

Disc golf discs are uniquely designed to achieve different flight paths, distances, and levels of control. Unlike traditional frisbees, which are built for casual tossing, disc golf discs are engineered for precision, speed, and stability. Players typically carry a mix of drivers, midranges, and putters, each serving a distinct role in their game. Understanding the differences between these disc types and when to use them can significantly improve a player's overall performance. Whether you are a beginner building your first disc selection or an experienced player refining your bag, choosing the right disc for the right shot is essential.

Drivers for distance, midranges for control, and putters for precision—each disc has a purpose.

A. Drivers: Maximum Distance and Speed

Drivers are designed for long-distance throws, making them essential for tee shots and fairway drives. Their thin rims and aerodynamic profiles allow them to travel farther than other disc types, but they also require proper form and arm speed to reach their full potential. Players looking to maximize distance should focus on developing clean throwing mechanics before relying on high-speed drivers.

- **Distance drivers** – Built for maximum speed and range, requiring significant power and technique to control. They typically have wider rims, allowing for high-speed flights. Ideal for long, open fairways where reaching maximum distance is key.

- **Fairway drivers** – Offer more control than distance drivers while still achieving solid distance. With slightly narrower rims, they provide better accuracy and are excellent for wooded courses, tight fairways, or players who prioritize precision over power.

Tips for Using Drivers Effectively

- **Arm speed is essential** – Use distance drivers only when you have the arm speed to control them. Throwing them too slowly can cause them to fade early and lose distance.

- **Fairway drivers for control** – Fairway drivers are excellent for beginners because they provide a mix of distance and control.

- **Consider wind conditions** – When playing on a windy day, overstable drivers tend to handle headwinds better, while understable drivers may turn too much.

B. Midrange Discs: Versatility and Control

Midrange discs are the most balanced and versatile option, offering a mix of distance, accuracy, and predictability. With thicker rims than drivers but thinner than putters, they are easier to control and less likely to turn over on release. Midranges are useful for a variety of shot types, making them an essential part of any player's disc selection.

- **Straight and stable flights** – Useful for approach shots, shorter drives, and controlled fairway play.

- **Easier to control** – Reduces the risk of errant throws and helps maintain consistency.

- **Beginner-friendly** – Ideal for learning proper throwing techniques due to their balanced flight characteristics.

When to Use a Midrange Disc

- **Navigating wooded areas** – Midranges offer better control than drivers, making them ideal for tight fairways where precision is more important than distance.

- **Approach shots** – Midranges provide predictable flights and are excellent for controlled landing near the basket.

- **Calm weather conditions** – These discs are less affected by wind than lightweight drivers, making them reliable in stable weather.

C. Putters: Precision for Close-Range Shots

Putters are the slowest and most controllable discs, designed for short-distance accuracy and minimal ground action. With their thicker, rounded rims, putters are comfortable to grip and offer consistent flights with limited fade. They play a crucial role in the short game, where precision is more important than distance.

- **Stable, predictable flights** – Hold their line well and resist excessive movement after landing.

- **Maximum control** – Ideal for short throws where accuracy is the top priority.

- **Helpful for form development** – Exaggerates inconsistencies in throwing technique, making them great for practice.

Tips for Using Putters Effectively

- **Use for both putting and approach shots** – Putters provide excellent accuracy for close-range throws.

- **Improve throwing technique** – Driving with putters helps develop smooth, controlled releases.

- **Consider multiple putters** – Having separate putters for putting and throwing approaches ensures more consistency in different shot situations.

D. Understanding Stability & Flight Paths

Stability is a key factor in determining how a disc will fly under normal throwing conditions. Each disc type can exhibit different stability characteristics, affecting flight paths and shot selection.

- **Overstable** – Fades to the left for right-hand backhand throws or to the right for left-hand backhand throws. Ideal for windy conditions and predictable hyzer shots.

- **Stable** – Flies mostly straight with minimal fade. Great for controlled and accurate throws.

- **Understable** – Turns to the right for right-hand backhand throws or to the left for left-hand backhand throws before fading. Useful for turnover shots, beginners, or lower arm speeds.

E. Building a Balanced Disc Selection

A well-rounded bag includes a mix of drivers, midranges, and putters, each suited to different situations. Carrying a variety of disc speeds and stability levels helps players adjust to different courses, conditions, and shot requirements.

- **Fairway and distance drivers** – A mix of slower and faster drivers provides both control and maximum distance potential.

- **Varied midranges** – Different midrange discs help handle a variety of approach shots and fairway plays.

- **Multiple putters** – Having separate putters for putting and throwing approaches ensures more consistency in different shot situations.

How to Build the Right Disc Selection

- **Start simple as a beginner** – Fairway drivers, a stable midrange, and a putter form a solid foundation before adding high-speed distance drivers.

- **Expand disc variety** – Experienced players benefit from carrying multiple versions of each disc type in different stability ratings.

- **Test different plastic types** – Finding the right disc feel and flight characteristics can be fine-tuned through various plastic blends and weights.

F. Key Takeaways

Disc golf discs fall into three main categories, each designed for specific distances and shot types. Drivers maximize speed and distance but require proper form to control. Midranges offer a balance of control and distance, making them ideal for approach shots and shorter drives. Putters provide the most accuracy and consistency for short-range throws and putting.

- **Drivers excel in distance** – Distance drivers maximize range, while fairway drivers provide better control on tighter lines.

- **Midranges offer versatility** – These discs balance accuracy and distance, making them useful for controlled fairway and approach shots.

- **Putters prioritize precision** – Slower speeds and stable flights make putters ideal for short-range accuracy and confidence in putting.

- **Stability affects flight paths** – Overstable discs fade more, stable discs fly straight, and understable discs turn before fading.

- **A balanced disc selection improves performance** – Carrying a variety of discs ensures adaptability to different course layouts and playing conditions.

Now that you understand disc types and their roles, the next section explores how to choose the right disc based on plastic types, weights, and flight ratings, helping players make informed decisions when selecting new discs.

2.2 Choosing the Right Disc: Plastic Types, Weights & Flight Ratings

Selecting the right disc goes beyond just picking a driver, midrange, or putter. Disc material, weight, and flight ratings all play a major role in how a disc performs on the course. Understanding these factors helps players make informed choices when expanding their bag, ensuring they have discs that match their skill level, throwing power, and course conditions. This section covers the key elements of disc selection, explaining how plastic types affect grip and durability, how disc weight influences control and flight, and how flight ratings provide insight into a disc's behavior in the air.

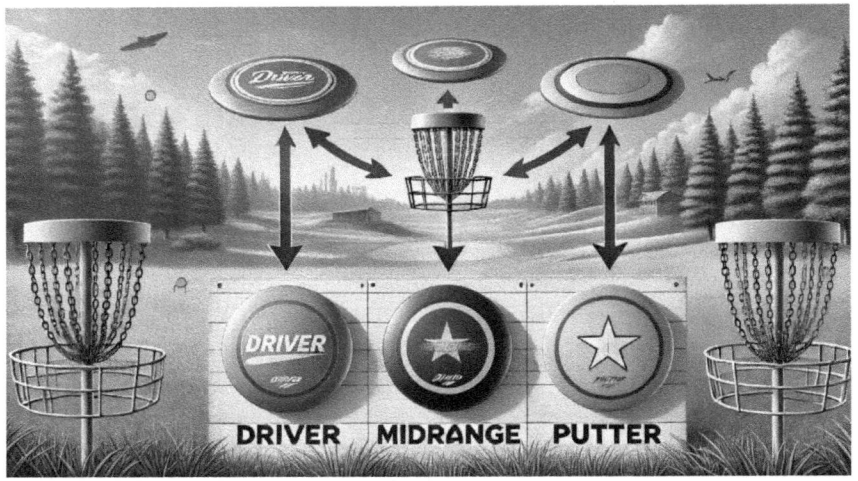

Understanding plastic types, weights, and flight ratings helps you select the perfect disc for your style.

A. Plastic Types: Grip, Durability & Performance

Disc manufacturers offer a wide variety of plastic blends, each designed to provide different levels of grip, flexibility, and durability. The choice of plastic can significantly impact how a disc flies, how well it holds up over time, and how comfortable it feels in the hand.

- **Base plastics** – Soft, affordable plastics with excellent grip but lower durability. They wear in quickly, which can change a disc's flight over time. Examples include Innova DX, Discraft Pro-D, and Latitude 64 Retro.

- **Mid-grade plastics** – A balance of grip and durability, providing a longer-lasting option that still maintains a good feel in the hand. Popular examples include Innova Pro, Discraft Elite-X, and Latitude 64 Tournament.

- **Premium plastics** – Highly durable and resistant to wear, making them ideal for long-term use. However, they may be slightly slicker, reducing grip in wet conditions. Examples include Innova Star, Discraft ESP, and Latitude 64 Gold Line.

- **Transparent & overstable plastics** – Some blends, like Innova Champion or Discraft Z, are highly durable but tend to be more overstable, meaning they fade harder at the end of their flight.

B. Disc Weight: How It Affects Flight & Control

Disc weight plays a crucial role in stability, distance, and control. Most discs range from 150 grams to 175 grams, though some putters and specialty discs can be heavier.

- **Lightweight discs (150-165g)** – Easier to throw with less effort, making them ideal for beginners, players with lower arm speed, and those throwing in tailwinds. Lighter discs tend to be more understable, turning more to the right for right-hand backhand (RHBH) throws.

- **Midweight discs (166-172g)** – A balance of distance and control, suitable for most players. These discs provide stability without requiring extreme arm speed.

- **Max weight discs (173-175g)** – Preferred by advanced players for increased predictability and wind resistance. Heavier discs resist turning over and tend to be more overstable.

C. Flight Ratings: Understanding Disc Flight Characteristics

Every disc is assigned a flight rating system that helps players predict its flight path. The most common rating system, developed by Innova, consists of four numbers: speed, glide, turn, and fade.

- **Speed (1-14)** – Measures how fast a disc must be thrown to achieve its intended flight. Higher-speed discs (10-14) require more power, while lower-speed discs (1-7) are easier to control.

- **Glide (1-7)** – Determines how well a disc stays in the air. Higher glide (5-7) is great for distance, while lower glide (1-3) offers more control.

- **Turn (+1 to -5)** – Indicates how much a disc turns to the right (RHBH) during high-speed flight. More negative numbers (-3 to -5) mean more turn, while positive numbers (+1) indicate stability.

- **Fade (0-5)** – Shows how much a disc fades left (RHBH) at the end of its flight. A fade of 0-1 finishes straight, while a fade of 4-5 hooks sharply left.

D. Matching Discs to Your Playing Style

Every player has a unique arm speed, throwing angle, and power level, meaning the same disc may fly differently for different people. Choosing discs that complement your playing style is key to consistency and improvement.

- **Lower-speed discs (5-9) are best for beginners** – These provide easier control and longer flights without requiring high arm speed.

- **Understable discs (-2 to -4 turn) work well for lower arm speeds** – They allow for smoother, straighter flights rather than fading out early.

- **Overstable discs (higher fade ratings) are best for windy conditions** – These provide predictable flights that resist turning over in strong winds.

- **Testing different plastic blends and weights helps fine-tune disc selection** – Players can experiment to find discs that match their grip preference and throwing style.

- **Fairway drivers are a great starting point** – They offer a balance of control and distance, making them ideal for players transitioning from midranges to drivers.

- **Max-weight putters and midranges improve accuracy** – Using heavier putters for short-range shots helps maintain precision and consistency.

- **Distance drivers should be introduced gradually** – Players should develop good technique before adding high-speed drivers to their bag.

E. How Disc Wear Affects Flight

Over time, discs wear down due to repeated throws, tree hits, and course conditions. As they wear in, their flight characteristics can change, often making them more understable. Understanding how wear affects discs helps players adjust their bag accordingly.

- **New discs maintain their original stability** – Fresh out of the package, discs fly according to their flight ratings.

- **Worn-in discs become more understable** – A once-stable disc may start turning more to the right (RHBH) as it wears.

- **Beat-in putters and midranges offer straighter flights** – Many players prefer worn-in putters for approaches because they hold a straighter line.

- **Overstable drivers become more versatile** – As an overstable disc wears in, it can be used for turnover shots or longer glide.

- **Rotating discs helps manage wear** – Carrying multiple versions of the same disc in different wear stages ensures a variety of flight paths.

F. Key Takeaways

Choosing the right disc involves understanding plastic types, weights, and flight ratings. Different plastic blends affect grip, durability, and stability, while disc weight influences flight control and wind resistance. Flight ratings help players predict how a disc will behave in the air, allowing for better shot selection on the course.

- **Plastic types impact grip and durability** – Base plastics provide better grip, while premium plastics last longer but may feel slicker.

- **Disc weight influences stability and flight** – Lighter discs offer more distance but less control, while heavier discs provide better consistency, especially in wind.

- **Flight ratings help determine disc behavior** – Speed, glide, turn, and fade numbers guide players in selecting the right disc for their skill level.

- **Players should match discs to their throwing style** – Selecting discs that complement arm speed, power, and course conditions leads to better overall performance.

- **Disc wear affects flight over time** – Worn-in discs become more understable, which can be useful for specific shot types.

Now that you know how to select the right discs, the next section explores must-have accessories that can enhance convenience, organization, and overall performance on the course.

2.3 Must-Have Accessories: Bags, Mini Markers, Towels & More

While discs are the most essential part of the game, having the right accessories enhances organization, improves comfort, and makes rounds more efficient. The right gear ensures players can focus on performance rather than minor inconveniences, leading to a smoother and more enjoyable experience. Whether it's carrying discs with ease, maintaining grip in varying weather conditions, or staying hydrated for endurance, accessories play a key role in optimizing gameplay. This section covers disc golf bags for carrying gear, mini markers for tournament play, towels and grip aids for better control, hydration and snacks for sustained energy, and additional tools that improve the playing experience.

**A well-stocked bag keeps you prepared for every round—
organization is key.**

A. Disc Golf Bags: Carrying Gear with Ease

A disc golf bag is essential for keeping gear organized and accessible
throughout a round. Whether a player carries only a few discs or an
entire selection, the right bag can improve convenience and reduce
strain. Various types of disc golf bags cater to different needs, from
casual play to high-level tournaments, making it important to choose
one that best fits a player's playing style and comfort preferences.
Investing in a high-quality bag ensures durability and longevity,
preventing unnecessary replacements over time.

- **Small starter bags** – Compact and lightweight, ideal for
  beginners or casual rounds with a few discs.

- **Medium shoulder bags** – Offers more storage while
  remaining portable, great for players transitioning to more
  serious play.

- **Backpacks** – Preferred by competitive players, providing
  maximum space, ergonomic comfort, and durability.

- **Cart-based bags** – Designed for tournament players who
  prefer rolling their gear instead of carrying it.

- **Comfortable straps** – Reduces strain on shoulders and back during long rounds.

- **Multiple compartments** – Offers space for discs, drinks, towels, scorecards, and personal items.

- **Durability** – Protects discs and gear in various playing conditions.

- **Lightweight design** – Helps prevent fatigue while walking the course.

B. Mini Markers: Essential for Tournament Play

Mini markers are a small yet crucial accessory for both casual and competitive play. In PDGA-sanctioned tournaments, they are required for marking a player's lie before their next throw, ensuring that every shot follows the official rules. Even outside of tournaments, using mini markers helps maintain proper positioning and consistency, making them a valuable addition to any player's bag. They also provide a small but meaningful way for players to express personality, as they come in a variety of custom designs and colors.

- **Marking the lie** – Ensures proper placement before taking the next throw.

- **Preventing violations** – Helps maintain fair play by marking disc locations accurately.

- **Customization** – Available in various designs, adding a personal touch while remaining functional.

C. Towels & Grip Aids: Staying Dry for Consistent Throws

Weather conditions can significantly impact grip, making towels and grip aids an essential part of a disc golfer's gear. Whether playing in hot, humid weather or wet, rainy conditions, maintaining a secure grip on the disc is key to consistent throwing. Various towels and grip-enhancing products help players manage moisture and improve control throughout their rounds. Keeping multiple towels in a bag ensures players are prepared for changing conditions, especially in tournaments or long rounds.

- **Microfiber towels** – Highly absorbent and fast-drying, ideal for keeping hands and discs dry.

- **Cotton towels** – More affordable but take longer to dry, making them useful for wiping dirt and mud off discs.

- **Grip bags** – Small pouches filled with chalk or rosin to absorb moisture and improve grip consistency.

- **Birdie bags** – A popular choice for players who want a dry grip without leaving residue on their discs.

- **Towel placement** – Keeping a towel clipped to a bag or belt loop allows quick access between throws.

D. Hydration & Snacks: Staying Energized on the Course

Playing a full round of disc golf requires endurance and focus, which makes hydration and nutrition essential. Many courses do not have water stations, so bringing personal drinks and snacks helps players maintain energy and prevent fatigue. Having the right refreshments on hand allows players to stay mentally sharp and physically prepared for the duration of the game. Staying hydrated is especially critical in warmer climates or during summer months when excessive sweating can lead to dehydration.

- **Water bottles** – Staying hydrated is key for peak performance and stamina.

- **Energy-boosting snacks** – Foods like granola bars, trail mix, or fruit provide quick, sustained energy without being too heavy.

- **Avoiding heavy meals** – Large meals before playing can cause sluggishness and discomfort.

- **Electrolyte drinks** – Helpful on hot days to replenish lost minerals and prevent dehydration.

- **Insulated bottles** – Keeps drinks cold throughout the round.

E. Additional Accessories for a Better Playing Experience

Beyond the essentials, several extra accessories can enhance a player's experience on the course. These tools improve convenience, comfort, and efficiency, helping players navigate obstacles, track scores, and prepare for varying weather conditions. While not mandatory, they provide added benefits that can make each round smoother and more enjoyable. Carrying a few extra items in a bag can be the difference between a frustrating round and a well-prepared, enjoyable game.

- **Retrievers** – Extendable tools designed to recover discs from water hazards, trees, or difficult terrain.

- **Scorecards & apps** – Paper scorecards or apps like UDisc help track scores, statistics, and course layouts.

- **Sunglasses & hats** – Protect against glare and sun exposure during long rounds.

- **First aid kits** – Useful for minor scrapes, insect bites, or other small injuries that may occur on the course.

- **Rain gear** – Umbrellas, rain jackets, or waterproof bags help players stay dry and comfortable in wet conditions.

- **Cold-weather gear** – Hand warmers, gloves, and layered clothing keep players warm in winter rounds.

F. Key Takeaways

Disc golf accessories help players stay organized, comfortable, and prepared for any playing conditions.

- **Disc golf bags** – Provide storage and accessibility, helping players carry gear efficiently.

- **Mini markers** – Necessary for proper lie placement, ensuring fair play in tournaments and casual rounds.

- **Towels and grip aids** – Help maintain control, preventing slippage in humid or rainy conditions.

- **Hydration and snacks** – Support endurance and concentration, allowing players to maintain performance over long rounds.

- **Additional accessories** – Retrievers, scorecards, and sunglasses add convenience, making each round more enjoyable.

With the right accessories, players can focus on improving their skills and having fun on the course. The next section explores the best footwear and apparel choices for stability, comfort, and performance in all playing conditions.

2.4 What to Wear: Best Shoes & Apparel for Performance

Wearing the right gear in disc golf is just as important as having the right discs. Proper footwear and apparel enhance comfort, stability, and performance, allowing players to focus on their throws without distractions. Disc golf courses vary in terrain, from wooded trails to open fields, requiring appropriate shoes for traction and clothing for weather adaptability. Selecting the right gear ensures better endurance, safety, and consistency throughout a round. Additionally, having the right accessories, such as hats, gloves, and compression gear, can improve comfort and performance in various playing conditions.

The right apparel and footwear provide comfort, stability, and grip for all conditions.

A. Best Shoes for Disc Golf: Traction, Stability & Comfort

Footwear plays a vital role in disc golf, providing the necessary grip and support for controlled movements and powerful throws. Since courses often feature uneven terrain, wet grass, and rocky paths, choosing shoes designed for traction and durability can prevent slips and improve overall balance. The right shoes also reduce foot fatigue, helping players maintain energy during long rounds. Proper footwear is especially crucial for players who compete regularly, as playing multiple rounds a day can put significant stress on the feet and lower body.

- **Hiking shoes & trail runners** – Offer excellent grip, ankle support, and durability, making them ideal for rough terrain and wooded courses. Their aggressive tread patterns provide stability for uneven surfaces.

- **Turf shoes** – Designed for grass fields, these shoes offer lightweight comfort and traction. They work well on dry courses but may lack durability for rugged conditions.

- **Waterproof shoes** – Essential for playing in wet or muddy conditions, keeping feet dry and preventing discomfort. Some models include breathable membranes to maintain airflow while repelling moisture.

- **Casual athletic shoes** – Suitable for short rounds or beginner players but may lack the grip and support needed for competitive play. These shoes can lead to slipping or instability on uneven terrain.

Key Features to Look for in Disc Golf Shoes

- **Strong grip & tread patterns** – Prevents slipping on wet or uneven surfaces. Look for aggressive treads that offer multi-directional traction.

- **Durability & weather resistance** – Ensures long-lasting performance in different conditions, especially on wooded or hilly courses.

- **Comfortable fit & arch support** – Reduces foot fatigue during long rounds, allowing players to focus on their game rather than discomfort.

- **Breathable materials** – Helps keep feet cool and dry in warm weather while reducing sweat buildup.

B. Apparel for Disc Golf: Comfort & Functionality

Disc golf clothing should be flexible, breathable, and appropriate for varying weather conditions. Since players engage in constant movement, twisting, and bending, wearing gear that allows unrestricted motion is crucial. Selecting lightweight and moisture-wicking fabrics improves comfort and helps maintain focus on performance. Proper apparel also provides protection against the elements, ensuring that players can compete comfortably regardless of the season.

- **Moisture-wicking shirts** – Keeps sweat away from the skin, preventing discomfort and overheating in warm weather. Dri-fit and polyester blends are commonly used for breathability.

- **Lightweight shorts or athletic pants** – Allow for unrestricted movement while providing comfort. Materials should be flexible without being too loose or restrictive.

- **Compression sleeves or leggings** – Offer additional support, improve circulation, and help reduce muscle fatigue, particularly in colder weather.

- **Weather-resistant jackets** – Protect against rain and wind without restricting mobility. A lightweight, packable option is ideal for unpredictable conditions.

- **Hats & sunglasses** – Shield against sun glare and excessive heat, improving visibility and reducing eye strain during play.

Dressing for Different Weather Conditions

- **Hot weather** – Opt for light, breathable fabrics to stay cool and prevent overheating. Loose-fitting clothing made of moisture-wicking material can help maintain comfort.

- **Cold weather** – Layer up with insulated clothing while maintaining flexibility for throws. Base layers made of thermal or compression materials work best for retaining warmth without restricting motion.

- **Rainy conditions** – Wear waterproof outer layers to stay dry without restricting movement. Water-resistant jackets, pants, and shoes are recommended for keeping dry.

- **Windy conditions** – Choose snug-fitting clothing that won't interfere with throwing mechanics. Loose clothing can create drag, affecting balance and release timing.

C. Additional Accessories for Enhanced Performance

Beyond shoes and apparel, certain accessories can improve comfort, grip, and endurance on the course. These small additions can help players maintain better grip, prevent injuries, and improve overall endurance. Accessories like gloves and knee braces also provide extra support, reducing the risk of injury and enhancing stability during play.

- **Gloves** – Useful in cold or wet weather to maintain grip and warmth. Some players prefer gloves for extra traction, especially in damp conditions.

- **Knee braces & ankle supports** – Provide extra stability for players who need additional joint protection. This can help prevent injuries and improve confidence on uneven terrain.

- **Sunscreen & bug spray** – Helps prevent sunburn and insect bites, especially on wooded courses where mosquitoes and ticks may be present.

- **Sweatbands & wristbands** – Keeps hands dry for a more secure grip on the disc. These are particularly useful in humid conditions to prevent sweat from affecting throwing form.

- **Hand warmers** – Helpful in cold conditions to keep hands warm and flexible, ensuring better grip and control during throws.

- **Neck gaiters & beanies** – Provide extra warmth for winter play while remaining lightweight and non-restrictive.

D. Key Takeaways

Wearing the right shoes and clothing is essential for comfort, stability, and performance in disc golf.

- **Disc golf shoes** – Hiking shoes, trail runners, and waterproof options provide the best traction, durability, and support for different course conditions.

- **Moisture-wicking apparel** – Lightweight, breathable fabrics keep players comfortable in hot weather, while layered clothing helps retain warmth in colder conditions.

- **Weather-specific gear** – Waterproof jackets, wind-resistant clothing, and insulated layers allow players to adapt to changing conditions.

- **Essential accessories** – Gloves, knee braces, and wristbands enhance grip, prevent injuries, and improve overall comfort on the course.

- **Sun protection** – Hats, sunglasses, and sunscreen help players stay protected from sun exposure, improving visibility and endurance.

By dressing for the conditions and choosing gear that supports movement and stability, players can focus more on their game and less on discomfort, improving their overall disc golf experience. The next chapter explores disc golf course design and layout, helping players navigate and strategize for different terrains and challenges.

Chapter 2 Review: Essential Disc Golf Gear

Chapter 2 provides a complete guide to the essential gear needed for disc golf, covering disc types, how to select the right one, must-have accessories, and proper clothing and footwear. Choosing the right equipment helps players optimize their game, stay comfortable on the course, and improve their overall experience.

2.1 Disc Types: Drivers, Midranges & Putters Explained

- **Drivers** – Designed for speed and distance, ideal for long throws. Distance drivers require high arm speed, while fairway drivers offer more control.

- **Midrange discs** – Balanced and versatile, providing accuracy and consistency for shorter drives and approach shots. Easier to control, making them great for beginners.

- **Putters** – The slowest and most accurate discs, essential for controlled putts and short approach shots. Their stable flight path makes them reliable for precision throws.

- **Understanding flight characteristics** – Stability, weight, and plastic type affect a disc's behavior, helping players make better shot selections.

2.2 Choosing the Right Disc: Plastic Types, Weights & Flight Ratings

- **Plastic types** – Grip, durability, and disc stability vary by material. Base plastics provide better grip but wear quickly, while premium plastics last longer.

- **Disc weight** – Lighter discs require less power, making them easier for beginners, while heavier discs offer better wind resistance and stability.

- **Flight ratings** – Speed, glide, turn, and fade determine how a disc flies. Understanding these factors helps players choose discs suited to their throwing style.

- **Building a balanced bag** – A mix of drivers, midranges, and putters ensures versatility for different shot types.

2.3 Must-Have Accessories: Bags, Mini Markers, Towels & More

- **Disc golf bags** – Available in small, medium, and large sizes, helping players organize and carry discs efficiently.

- **Mini markers** – Used to mark a disc's lie during play, required in tournaments but useful in casual rounds.

- **Towels & grip aids** – Keeping hands and discs dry improves grip and consistency, especially in humid or wet conditions.

- **Hydration & snacks** – Staying hydrated and fueled with light snacks helps maintain energy and endurance.

- **Additional accessories** – Retrievers for lost discs, sunglasses for sun protection, and scorecards or apps for tracking performance.

2.4 What to Wear: Best Shoes & Apparel for Performance

- **Footwear choices** – Hiking shoes and trail runners provide traction and durability, while waterproof shoes help in wet conditions.

- **Clothing recommendations** – Moisture-wicking shirts, flexible athletic wear, and weather-resistant jackets keep players comfortable.

- **Weather considerations** – Dressing appropriately for hot, cold, rainy, or windy weather enhances comfort and playability.

- **Extra gear** – Items like gloves, knee braces, sunscreen, and sweatbands improve comfort and endurance.

Chapter 2 ensures players have the right gear for a better playing experience. The next chapter explores disc golf course layouts and design, helping players navigate different course types and terrains effectively.

Chapter 3: Disc Golf Course Layout & Design

Disc golf courses vary widely in design, each presenting unique challenges that test a player's skill, strategy, and adaptability. Understanding course elements—tee pads, fairways, baskets, and hazards—helps players make smarter shot selections. This chapter explores the key components of a course, different layouts suited for various skill levels, and how to adjust to changing terrain and elevation. You'll also learn strategies for navigating obstacles, mandatories, and out-of-bounds areas to improve accuracy and course management. Mastering these concepts allows players to read the course effectively, anticipate challenges, and confidently approach each round with a strategic mindset.

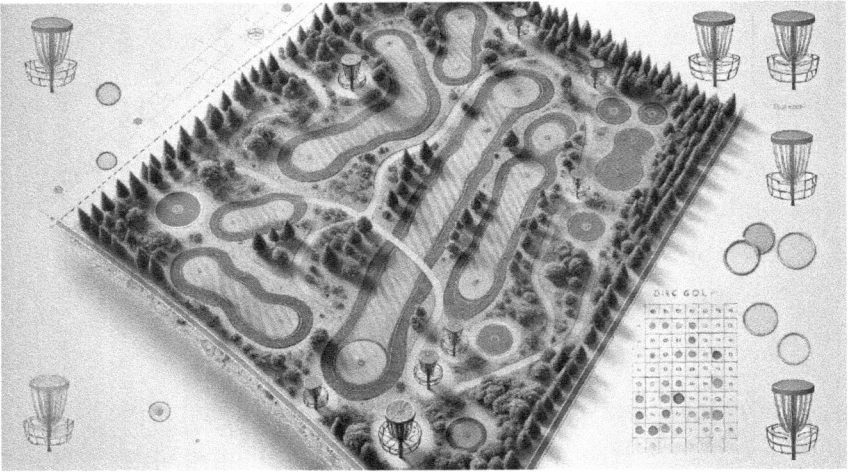

A well-designed course challenges players of all skill levels—learn to read and adapt to any layout.

3.1 Understanding Course Elements: Tees, Fairways & Baskets

Every disc golf course consists of fundamental elements that shape how a round is played. Tees, fairways, and baskets serve as the primary components of each hole, influencing shot selection, difficulty, and overall strategy. Understanding these course elements helps players read the layout effectively, plan their throws, and adjust their game to different challenges. Whether navigating a tight wooded fairway, approaching a guarded basket, or choosing the best stance on a tee pad, knowing how each component impacts play is essential for improving performance. Additionally, recognizing how course design elements influence the game allows players to develop a strategic mindset, helping them anticipate challenges before stepping up to throw.

Recognizing tees, fairways, and baskets helps you navigate any course effectively.

A. Tee Pads: The Starting Point of Every Hole

The tee pad is where every hole begins, setting the foundation for the first throw. A solid and consistent tee pad allows players to generate power while maintaining balance and control. The quality and design of a tee pad can significantly impact a player's ability to execute a clean drive. Factors such as length, surface material, and elevation all contribute to how comfortable and effective a player's run-up and release will be.

- **Concrete tee pads** – The most common and durable option, providing a firm surface for consistent footing. They allow for strong run-ups but may become slick when wet.

- **Rubber or turf tee pads** – Offer good traction while being softer on the joints, commonly used on courses where concrete isn't feasible. Turf pads provide a natural feel, while rubber mats offer a grip-enhancing surface.

- **Natural tee areas** – Some courses use dirt or grass tees, which can be less stable and affected by weather conditions, making them inconsistent over time.

How Tee Pads Affect Throwing Technique

- **Grip and stability** – A good tee pad provides enough traction to prevent slipping while allowing players to pivot smoothly.

- **Run-up space** – Longer pads give players more room for a full approach, while shorter ones require a controlled, compact form.

- **Elevation and angles** – Some tee pads are sloped or positioned on raised platforms, requiring adjustments to stance and throwing motion.

B. Fairways: The Path to the Basket

A fairway is the playing area between the tee pad and the basket, designed to challenge players with a variety of obstacles and shot choices. Course designers use fairways to shape the playing experience, testing a player's ability to control distance, accuracy, and disc flight. Understanding the type of fairway a hole presents allows players to make better shot selections, adjusting their approach to maximize scoring opportunities.

- **Open fairways** – Wide, unobstructed spaces that favor power throws and distance drivers. These holes often allow players to focus on maximizing distance but may require precise shot placement for an ideal approach.

- **Wooded fairways** – Narrow, technical layouts requiring controlled shots, shot-shaping, and strategic disc selection. Players must navigate trees and gaps, often relying on midrange discs or fairway drivers for accuracy.

- **Elevated fairways** – Uphill and downhill slopes that impact disc stability and flight path, requiring players to adjust their angles and power. Uphill shots demand more force to counteract gravity, while downhill shots can gain unexpected speed and distance.

Fairway Strategies for Success

- **Shot shaping** – Understanding how to control hyzer and anhyzer angles helps players navigate trees and doglegs effectively.

- **Disc selection** – Stable discs are better for straight and predictable flights, while overstable discs handle windy conditions and fade more reliably.

- **Playing to landing zones** – Instead of always aiming for max distance, positioning the disc for an easier approach shot can lower scores.

C. Baskets: The Target and Scoring Zone

The basket is the ultimate goal on every hole, serving as the target where players complete their throws. Modern disc golf baskets are designed with metal chains to absorb impact and catch the disc, preventing excessive rollaways. However, basket positioning, elevation, and environmental factors can all impact putting success. Being aware of these factors allows players to approach the basket with confidence, adjusting their putting style to improve accuracy.

- **Standard PDGA-approved baskets** – Feature a metal chain assembly and a lower tray to securely hold discs. These are used in all competitive settings.

- **Portable baskets** – Lighter and more flexible, often used for practice or temporary courses. These may not catch as effectively as permanent course baskets.

- **Elevated baskets** – Positioned on mounds or raised platforms to add difficulty and require precise putting. These often appear on championship-level courses.

- **Hanging baskets** – Suspended from trees or structures, introducing movement and unpredictability to putts.

Basket Positioning & Putting Strategies

- **Guarded baskets** – Placed near trees, bushes, or rocks, forcing players to shape their approaches carefully.

- **Slope considerations** – Baskets on hills increase the risk of rollaways, requiring players to adjust their putting stance and aim for flatter landings.

- **Wind effects** – Wind can significantly alter putting accuracy, making spin putts or low-line putts more effective in gusty conditions.

D. Key Takeaways

A well-designed disc golf hole consists of a tee pad for a stable starting point, a fairway that presents strategic challenges, and a basket that requires accuracy to finish. Different tee surfaces, varying fairway types, and diverse basket placements all impact how a hole plays, requiring players to adjust their approach based on the course layout.

- **Tee pads** affect balance, power, and footwork, making it important to adjust for different surfaces.

- **Fairways** vary from open spaces to heavily wooded areas, requiring smart shot selection and risk assessment.

- **Baskets** come in different styles and placements, demanding adaptability in putting techniques and approach shots.

- **Environmental factors** – Wind, elevation, and ground conditions influence every shot and should be considered when planning throws.

- **Strategic play** – Choosing landing zones, avoiding hazards, and executing controlled approaches lead to better scores and consistency.

Mastering these course elements helps players make smarter decisions, improve shot execution, and develop a deeper understanding of how to navigate a round effectively. The next section explores the different types of courses, from beginner-friendly layouts to championship-level designs, helping players understand what to expect at various skill levels.

3.2 Types of Courses: Beginner, Intermediate & Championship Layouts

Disc golf courses come in a variety of layouts, each designed to challenge players at different skill levels. Some courses are beginner-friendly, featuring short distances and open fairways, while others cater to advanced players with long holes, technical fairways, and strategic shot requirements. Understanding the different course types helps players choose the right challenge, refine their strategy, and prepare for competitive play. Playing on a mix of courses improves adaptability, allowing players to develop well-rounded skills. This section explores the characteristics of beginner, intermediate, and championship-level courses, along with special course features that add variety and challenge to the game.

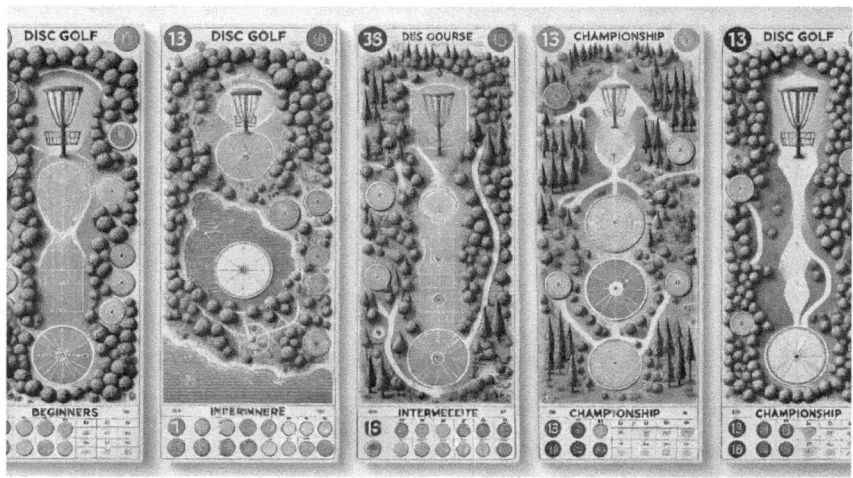

Every course offers a different challenge—choose one that matches your skill level.

A. Beginner Courses: Short, Simple & Accessible

Beginner courses are designed to introduce new players to disc golf in an enjoyable and stress-free way. These courses focus on accessibility, offering a welcoming environment for those developing their skills. With shorter hole distances, minimal obstacles, and straightforward layouts, they allow players to practice fundamental throwing techniques without frustration. Many beginner courses are located in public parks, making them easy to access and a great option for casual rounds or family outings.

- **Shorter hole distances** – Most holes range from 150 to 250 feet, allowing players to reach the basket in fewer throws.

- **Wide open fairways** – Fewer trees and obstacles reduce frustration and allow beginners to focus on throwing mechanics.

- **Flat terrain** – Minimal elevation changes make it easier to control throws and practice accuracy.

- **Straightforward basket placements** – Baskets are visible from the tee, eliminating the need for complex shot-shaping.

B. Intermediate Courses: Balanced Challenge & Variety

Intermediate courses offer a balance of challenge and accessibility, making them ideal for players looking to improve their game. These courses introduce more demanding fairways, requiring better shot control and strategic thinking. While still approachable for casual players, intermediate layouts encourage skill development by incorporating more obstacles, elevation changes, and varied hole designs. Playing these courses helps players refine their technique and prepare for more advanced competition.

- **Longer hole distances** – Holes range from 250 to 400 feet, requiring controlled drives and precise approach shots.

- **Moderate obstacles** – Trees, elevation changes, and occasional water hazards challenge shot placement without overwhelming players.

- **Varied fairways** – Some holes are open, while others require navigating wooded areas or doglegs.
- **More difficult basket placements** – Some baskets may be positioned on hills, near obstacles, or surrounded by hazards, requiring thoughtful approaches.

C. Championship Courses: Professional-Level Challenge & Strategy

Championship courses are designed for experienced players, offering the highest level of difficulty and requiring advanced skills. These courses feature long distances, technical fairways, and complex basket placements that test accuracy, power, and mental toughness. Many championship layouts are used in professional tournaments, emphasizing strategic play and consistency. Successfully navigating these courses requires not only precise throwing mechanics but also a deep understanding of shot selection and risk management.

- **Long hole distances** – Many holes exceed 400 feet, with par 4 or par 5 layouts demanding multiple precision shots.
- **Tightly wooded or technical fairways** – Players must navigate narrow gaps, execute controlled throws, and shape shots effectively.
- **Severe elevation changes** – Uphill and downhill holes require adjustments to throwing angles and power.
- **Difficult basket placements** – Baskets may be near cliffs, water hazards, or within tight tree clusters, making putting more challenging.
- **Mandatory routes (Mandos) & out-of-bounds (OB) areas** – Mandos force players to shape specific shots, while OB areas penalize errant throws.

D. Special Course Features & Alternative Layouts

Many disc golf courses incorporate unique features that add an extra layer of challenge and variety to the game. These special course elements create a dynamic playing experience and encourage players to adapt their strategies to different conditions. Some courses integrate multiple design elements, blending technical wooded holes with wide-open fairways or incorporating natural terrain features to shape the layout. These features make every round feel unique, even when playing the same course multiple times.

- **Hybrid courses** – Some courses combine open and wooded sections, providing a mix of different shot requirements.

- **Multiple tee pads & basket placements** – Many courses have different tees or basket locations to accommodate players of varying skill levels.

- **Water hazards** – Some layouts emphasize water features, requiring careful risk assessment and precision to avoid penalties.

- **Safari layouts** – Some courses allow players to create custom holes by playing to different baskets or extending hole distances.

- **Wind-exposed courses** – Coastal or mountain courses can add an extra challenge due to unpredictable wind conditions.

E. The Role of Course Design in Skill Development

Playing different types of courses plays a crucial role in a player's growth and development. Each course layout presents unique challenges that require players to refine their technique, decision-making, and adaptability. Beginner courses focus on developing the basics, while intermediate and championship courses introduce more complex obstacles, distances, and shot requirements. By regularly playing a variety of course styles, players gain experience in different environments, helping them become more confident and prepared for competition.

- **Beginner courses** build confidence by focusing on shorter holes, minimal obstacles, and a forgiving layout for developing fundamental throwing techniques.

- **Intermediate courses** refine shot selection, power control, and strategic play by introducing longer holes, tighter fairways, and more complex basket placements.

- **Championship courses** challenge advanced players with technical fairways, elevation changes, and high-pressure shots that demand precision, mental resilience, and consistency.

F. Key Takeaways

Disc golf courses vary in difficulty, design, and features, shaping a player's ability to develop new skills and refine their game.

- **Beginner courses** offer short distances and minimal obstacles, helping new players build confidence and improve their throwing form.

- **Intermediate courses** introduce more technical fairways and strategic basket placements, requiring players to refine shot control and decision-making.

- **Championship courses** demand precision, power, and mental toughness, testing players with long distances, elevation changes, and high-risk shot selections.

- **Unique course features** such as water hazards, multiple tee pads, and safari layouts create dynamic playing experiences that challenge adaptability.

- **Playing on a variety of courses** builds well-rounded skills, preparing players for different competitive levels and course conditions.

Understanding course design allows players to select the right challenges and develop a more strategic approach to the game. The next section explores how different terrains, from wooded forests to open fields, influence gameplay and shot execution.

3.3 Playing Different Terrains: Woods, Open Fields & Elevation Changes

Disc golf courses feature a variety of terrains, each presenting unique challenges that require players to adjust their throwing techniques and strategies. Some courses are carved through dense forests, demanding precision and control, while others feature wide-open fields where wind conditions play a major role. Elevation changes add another layer of complexity, affecting disc stability, distance control, and shot selection. Learning how to navigate different terrains effectively allows players to improve their game, make smarter decisions, and develop a well-rounded skill set. By practicing on various terrains, players enhance their adaptability and confidence across all course types.

Every terrain presents a new challenge—adjust your throws and strategies accordingly.

A. Playing in Wooded Courses: Precision & Shot Shaping

Wooded courses challenge players with tight fairways, narrow gaps, and natural obstacles that demand accuracy and control. Instead of relying on pure distance, players must focus on shot shaping, disc selection, and careful placement. Success in wooded courses often depends on maintaining composure, hitting precise lines, and making smart recovery shots when necessary.

- **Narrow fairways** – Trees and natural obstacles force players to shape their shots carefully, making controlled midrange throws and putters essential.

- **Low ceilings** – Overhanging branches limit throwing angles, requiring flatter releases and lower-trajectory shots to avoid hitting trees.

- **Gap hitting** – Many holes require threading the disc through tight gaps, making accuracy and release point consistency critical.

- **Strategic scrambling** – Missed lines often result in difficult lies behind trees, forcing players to develop creative recovery shots.

Best Strategies for Wooded Courses

- **Use stable or understable discs** – Neutral or understable discs help with controlled, straight flights through tight lines.

- **Prioritize accuracy over power** – Slower throws reduce the risk of deflections and bad ricochets.

- **Develop a variety of shot shapes** – Hyzer flips, anhyzers, and forehands help navigate different fairway angles.

- **Stay in the fairway** – Placement is key; landing in a clear area is often better than trying to gain extra distance.

B. Playing in Open Field Courses: Distance & Wind Control

Open courses offer fewer physical obstacles but present challenges related to distance control, wind conditions, and ground play. These layouts often favor players who can throw long drives while maintaining accuracy. Since wind exposure is a key factor in open courses, understanding how to adjust for different wind patterns is essential for consistent performance.

- **Longer hole distances** – Many open courses feature holes exceeding 400 feet, favoring players with strong driving ability.

- **Wind exposure** – With fewer trees for protection, wind can significantly affect disc stability and flight paths.

- **More forgiving fairways** – Fewer obstacles mean fewer restrictions, allowing for greater flexibility in shot selection.

- **Skip shots and ground play** – Grass and dirt fairways influence how discs land, potentially leading to extra distance or unpredictable skips.

Best Strategies for Open Field Courses

- **Adjust for wind conditions** – Headwinds make discs turn more, while tailwinds reduce fade; understanding this helps with shot planning.

- **Use overstable discs in strong winds** – Overstable discs resist turning and hold their intended flight path better in gusty conditions.

- **Take advantage of skip shots** – Hard-packed ground can allow for extra distance if a disc is angled correctly upon landing.

- **Maximize distance but stay in bounds** – Longer holes tempt big throws, but maintaining control is more important than pure power.

C. Playing on Elevation Changes: Uphill & Downhill Adjustments

Elevation changes significantly affect disc flight, requiring players to adjust throwing power, release angles, and landing strategies. Uphill and downhill shots influence disc stability and trajectory, making adaptability a crucial skill when playing on hilly courses. Recognizing how elevation impacts shot execution helps players maintain control and avoid costly mistakes.

- **Uphill shots** – Discs tend to fade sooner and lose distance faster due to the incline, requiring extra power and stability.

- **Downhill shots** – Gravity extends flight time, often making discs travel farther and hold their angle longer than expected.

- **Side slopes** – Uneven terrain can cause awkward footing and lead to rollaways if a disc lands at the wrong angle.

- **Elevated baskets** – Baskets placed on mounds or raised platforms require precise putting to avoid long comeback putts.

Best Strategies for Elevation Changes

- **Add extra power on uphill shots** – Aim slightly higher and throw with more force to counteract the incline.

- **Control angles on downhill shots** – Lighter throws with more nose-down angles prevent excessive fade and distance overshoots.

- **Adjust footing for balance** – On sloped terrain, maintaining a strong stance helps prevent slipping and off-balance throws.

- **Plan safe landings** – Avoid landing a disc on edge on a hill, as it may roll away and cost extra strokes.

D. Weather Impact on Different Terrains

Weather conditions play a significant role in how different terrains behave. Wind, rain, and temperature changes require players to adapt their throwing techniques and course management strategies. Understanding these environmental factors allows players to maintain consistency and control regardless of the playing conditions.

- **Wind effects in open fields** – Headwinds, tailwinds, and crosswinds can drastically alter disc flight.

- **Rain in wooded courses** – Wet ground creates slick footing, and rain-soaked discs affect grip and release.

- **Cold temperatures and disc stability** – Discs become more overstable in cold conditions and lose some flexibility.

- **Hot conditions and endurance** – Heat can drain energy quickly, making hydration and pacing critical for performance.

E. The Importance of Terrain Adaptability

Success in disc golf isn't just about throwing skill—it's about adjusting to the unique challenges each course presents. Whether navigating tight wooded fairways, launching drives across open fields, or managing the complexities of elevation changes, players must refine their strategies to fit the terrain. The ability to adapt ensures consistency, confidence, and better overall performance in any playing environment.

- **Adaptability** – Adjusting to different terrains improves shot execution, decision-making, and overall gameplay.

- **Strategic shot selection** – Each type of course requires adjustments in power, accuracy, and disc selection.

- **Course experience** – Exposure to a variety of terrains enhances skill development and prepares players for competitive rounds.

F. Key Takeaways

Disc golf terrain plays a crucial role in shaping a player's game, influencing shot selection, strategy, and execution. Learning to adjust to different landscapes ensures consistency and confidence in all playing conditions.

- **Wooded courses** – Demand precision, shot shaping, and controlled throws to navigate tight fairways.

- **Open field courses** – Emphasize distance while requiring wind adjustments and strategic landings.

- **Elevation changes** – Affect disc flight, requiring power modifications and careful release angles.

- **Weather conditions** – Influence play, making adaptability crucial in competitive rounds.

By mastering different terrains, players develop a complete skill set, improving adaptability and confidence in any course setting. The next section explores course strategy, focusing on navigating hazards, mandatories, and out-of-bounds areas for smarter play.

3.4 Course Strategy: Navigating Hazards, Mandos & OB Lines

Disc golf courses are designed with intentional challenges that require strategic thinking, precise execution, and risk assessment. Hazards, mandatories (mandos), and out-of-bounds (OB) lines influence shot selection and force players to adapt their approach based on course design. Successfully managing these elements is key to lowering scores and avoiding unnecessary penalties. Understanding how to navigate hazards, comply with mando rules, and stay in bounds will help players develop a more calculated game plan and improve overall performance. A well-planned approach leads to greater consistency, allowing players to avoid costly mistakes and improve their competitive play.

Smart course management means knowing when to take risks and when to play it safe.

A. Common Hazards & How to Play Around Them

Hazards create obstacles that players must navigate while avoiding penalty strokes or difficult recovery shots. Some hazards impose direct penalties, while others create tricky lies that force creative shot-making. Managing hazards effectively requires strategic placement, shot selection, and an understanding of course conditions.

- **Water hazards** – Ponds, lakes, rivers, and creeks present one of the biggest risks on a course. A disc that lands in water is typically considered OB, resulting in a penalty stroke and requiring a rethrow from a designated drop zone or the previous lie.

- **Thick rough & dense foliage** – Some courses feature heavily wooded areas or tall grass that make retrieving and throwing from a lie difficult. These areas often require creative shot-making to escape while avoiding additional strokes.

- **Bunkers & sand traps** – Certain courses integrate golf-style sand traps as designated hazards, requiring specific throws or resulting in penalty strokes when landed in.

- **Wind-prone areas** – Open courses or holes near water experience unpredictable gusts, affecting disc stability and flight paths.

Best Strategies for Avoiding Hazards

- **Prioritize controlled placement** – Playing for a safer landing zone can be more beneficial than aggressively attacking the basket.

- **Use overstable discs in windy conditions** – These discs resist turning and hold a more predictable flight path.

- **Plan recovery shots in advance** – Practicing escape throws improves the ability to get out of hazards without compounding mistakes.

- **Factor in ground play** – Discs can skip or roll into hazards, so choosing the right landing angle is essential.

B. Mandos (Mandatories) & Their Strategic Impact

Mandos are course-design features that force players to shape specific shot paths, ensuring safety and adding technical difficulty. Players must comply with mando rules to avoid penalty strokes and rethrows, making precision and planning essential when playing holes with mandatories.

- **Single mandos** – The disc must pass to a designated side of an object, such as a tree or pole.

- **Double mandos** – Players must throw between two marked objects, often forming a narrow gap.

- **Tunnel mandos** – These force low or straight throws, preventing wide hyzers or high anhyzers.

Strategies for Handling Mandos

- **Visualize the intended flight path before throwing** – Knowing how to approach the mando helps in disc selection and shot shaping.

- **Favor accuracy over power** – Missing a mando results in a penalty stroke and a rethrow, so precise execution is more important than distance.

- **Use stable discs with predictable flight paths** – Discs with consistent fade ensure a higher success rate when navigating mandos.

- **Play safe when necessary** – Rather than risking a difficult shot, choosing a high-percentage play can prevent penalty strokes.

C. Out-of-Bounds (OB) Rules & Strategies

Out-of-bounds areas limit where discs can land and add penalty strokes for errant throws. OB zones are usually marked with ropes, painted lines, or natural barriers like roads and water. Staying in bounds is crucial for maintaining a strong score and avoiding unnecessary mistakes.

- **Water OB** – Many OB areas involve bodies of water, requiring careful shot placement to avoid penalties.

- **Roads & paved paths** – Hard surfaces, often marked as OB, require players to adjust their landing strategies.

- **Artificial OB zones** – Some courses introduce marked OB sections to increase difficulty and force controlled play.

Strategies for Staying in Bounds

- **Play conservative shots when OB is nearby** – Prioritizing accuracy over distance helps prevent penalty strokes.

- **Choose discs with reliable fades** – Overstable discs resist turning and help keep shots within bounds.

- **Factor in wind conditions** – Strong winds can push discs off course, so adjusting angles can prevent OB landings.

- **Know OB rules for each course** – Some courses allow rethrows from previous lies, while others enforce drop zones; understanding these rules improves strategic decision-making.

D. Risk vs. Reward: Making Smart Decisions on the Course

Every hole presents choices between aggressive and conservative play. Some shots offer high-reward opportunities but also carry significant risks, such as clearing a long water hazard or threading a tight mando gap. Proper risk management helps players maximize opportunities while minimizing mistakes.

- **High-risk shots** – These include long carries over water, tight mando shots, and OB-lined fairways where aggressive play could lead to penalty strokes.

- **Low-risk alternatives** – Laying up before a hazard or taking a safer fairway route may prevent lost strokes.

- **Course knowledge is key** – Players familiar with a course can make better strategic decisions about when to attack and when to play conservatively.

Course hazards, mandos, and OB lines add strategic complexity to disc golf, requiring smart decision-making and controlled shot execution. Mastering these elements helps players navigate obstacles efficiently and avoid unnecessary strokes.

- **Hazards** – Water, thick rough, and wind-prone areas challenge shot selection and recovery skills, demanding strategic placement.

- **Mandatories (mandos)** – These course rules force specific shot shapes, guiding play through designated routes and adding difficulty.

- **Out-of-bounds (OB) areas** – Landing OB results in penalty strokes, emphasizing the importance of accurate throws and smart course management.

- **Risk vs. reward** – Evaluating when to play aggressively versus taking a safer approach helps maintain consistency and avoid costly mistakes.

By mastering these course elements, players can navigate obstacles efficiently, reduce unnecessary strokes, and improve overall strategy. The next section explores course management techniques, helping players analyze fairways, adjust for conditions, and develop a winning game plan.

Chapter 3 Review: Disc Golf Course Layout & Design

Chapter 3 explores the structure and design of disc golf courses, helping players understand how different layouts, terrains, and course elements impact gameplay. Mastering course design concepts allows players to improve decision-making, shot selection, and overall performance on the course. Whether playing on a wooded, open, or mixed-terrain course, understanding these elements is essential for adapting to different layouts and improving overall play.

3.1 Understanding Course Elements: Tees, Fairways & Baskets

- **Tee pads** – The starting point of each hole, offering stability for throws. Concrete pads provide a firm surface, turf offers cushioning, and natural tee pads may vary in traction.

- **Fairways** – The main playing area leading to the basket, ranging from wide-open spaces to technical wooded paths. Recognizing fairway shapes helps with shot selection and execution.

- **Baskets** – The final target, equipped with metal chains to catch discs. Basket placement on slopes, near water, or behind obstacles increases difficulty and requires strategic putting.

3.2 Types of Courses: Beginner, Intermediate & Championship Layouts

- **Beginner courses** – Short, simple layouts with minimal hazards, ideal for new players developing basic throwing techniques.

- **Intermediate courses** – Feature longer holes, a mix of wooded and open fairways, and elevation changes that challenge accuracy and strategic decision-making.

- **Championship courses** – Designed for high-level competition, featuring extended distances, narrow landing zones, and complex basket placements requiring advanced skills and control.

3.3 Playing Different Terrains: Woods, Open Fields & Elevation Changes

- **Wooded courses** – Demand precision and controlled shots to navigate tight fairways and avoid trees.

- **Open field courses** – Emphasize distance but require wind management and awareness of ground play.

- **Elevation changes** – Uphill shots reduce distance, requiring extra power, while downhill shots increase glide and require controlled landings.

3.4 Course Strategy: Navigating Hazards, Mandos & OB Lines

- **Hazards** – Water, thick rough, and wind-exposed areas force players to adjust shot placement and minimize risk.

- **Mandatories (mandos)** – Course rules requiring discs to pass a specific side of an obstacle, forcing players to plan routes carefully.

- **Out-of-bounds (OB) areas** – Marked sections where landing results in penalties, requiring precision and calculated risks.

Chapter 3 provides a deeper understanding of course design, layout types, and strategies for navigating different terrains and obstacles. The next chapter shifts focus to advanced course management, teaching players how to analyze holes, adjust for weather conditions, and develop a winning strategy.

Part 2: Mastering Disc Golf Techniques

Refining your disc golf technique is key to improving accuracy, consistency, and performance. While understanding the game is important, true skill comes from mastering throwing mechanics and putting strategies. This section covers essential techniques, including proper grip, powerful backhand and forehand throws, and specialized overhand shots like thumbers and tomahawks. You'll also explore the biomechanics behind efficient throws, helping you generate power while maintaining control. Additionally, we'll break down the art of putting—an essential skill for lowering scores—by examining different styles, stances, and mental strategies for clutch moments. Whether you're fine-tuning your form or learning new techniques, developing proper mechanics will give you the confidence and consistency needed to excel on the course.

Chapter 4: The Fundamentals of Throwing

Throwing technique is the foundation of disc golf, influencing distance, accuracy, and consistency. Whether executing a powerful backhand drive, a controlled forehand flick, or an overhand throw, mastering mechanics is key to performance. This chapter covers essential techniques, starting with proper grip for maximum control. Players will learn how to generate power and accuracy with the backhand, when to use the forehand, and the benefits of overhand throws like thumbers and tomahawks. Biomechanics will also be explored to improve efficiency, refine form, and develop a more controlled throwing motion. By mastering these fundamentals, players can build a strong technical foundation and enhance their overall game.

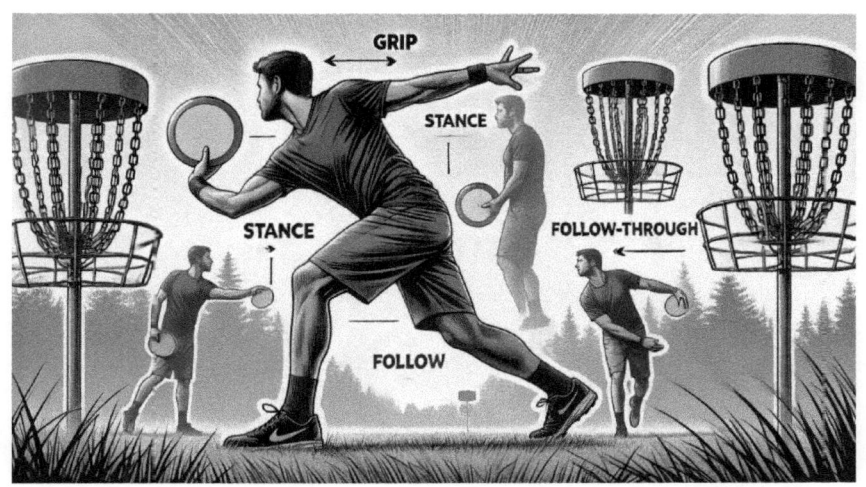

A strong foundation in grip, stance, and release is key to improving your disc golf throws.

4.1 Proper Grip Techniques for Maximum Control

Grip is one of the most fundamental aspects of disc golf, yet it is often overlooked despite its direct impact on performance. A proper grip provides control over the disc's release angle, spin, and flight path, making it essential for consistent and accurate throws. The way a player holds a disc influences their ability to execute different shot types, from power drives to finesse approaches and putts. Finding the right grip for various situations ensures better command over each throw and minimizes errors caused by poor hand positioning. This section explores key grip fundamentals, common grip types for backhand and forehand throws, and specialized grips for unique shot selections.

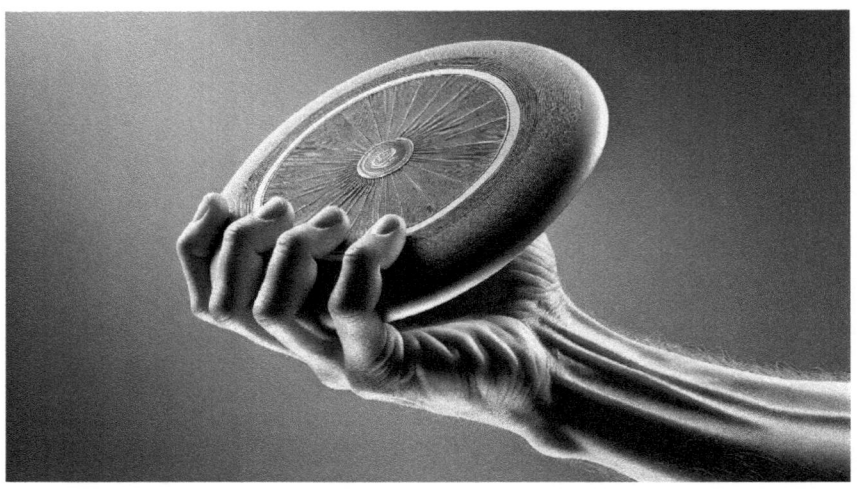

Finding the right grip gives you better control, accuracy, and confidence in every throw.

A. Key Factors in an Effective Grip

A proper grip should provide a balance between control, comfort, and release consistency. The way the fingers and thumb interact with the disc affects spin, stability, and shot execution. Too tight of a grip can result in grip lock, causing releases to be late, while a grip that's too loose may lead to slips or flutter in the flight path. Understanding the core elements of a good grip helps players avoid common mistakes and maximize their throwing potential.

- **Finger placement** – The positioning of fingers on the rim or underside of the disc determines stability and spin control. A proper setup ensures a clean release and minimizes unnecessary wobble.

- **Thumb pressure** – The thumb provides additional stability, controlling grip tightness and helping regulate release timing. Too much pressure can force early releases, while too little can cause slips.

- **Grip pressure** – Holding the disc too tightly can lead to inaccurate throws, while a weak grip can cause loss of control. Players should experiment with grip strength to find the right balance for different shot types.

B. Common Grips for Backhand Throws

Backhand throws are the most widely used shots in disc golf, requiring a grip that maximizes both power and accuracy. A secure grip allows for better control over spin and flight path, while different grip styles provide varying levels of stability and distance. Selecting the appropriate grip based on the shot type and disc stability helps players achieve more consistent results.

- **Power grip** – All four fingers are tucked tightly under the rim, generating maximum spin and distance. Ideal for long drives and high-speed shots.

- **Modified power grip** – Fingers are slightly spread under the rim, offering a balance of power and control. A great choice for accuracy while still maintaining distance.

- **Fan grip** – Fingers are spread along the underside of the disc, improving touch and precision. Often used for approach shots and putts.

- **Stacked grip** – Fingers rest on top of each other instead of being spread, providing a stable hold for midrange shots and controlled releases.

C. Common Grips for Forehand (Flick) Throws

Forehand throws require a grip that promotes wrist snap and disc stability. Unlike backhand grips, forehand grips rely more on wrist and finger positioning to generate spin and ensure a clean release. A proper forehand grip helps prevent wobbling and provides the necessary flick action for effective throws.

- **Two-finger forehand grip** – The index and middle fingers are placed along the inside rim of the disc, creating a firm grip for powerful wrist snaps.

- **Stacked forehand grip** – The index finger rests on top of the middle finger, providing extra control and reducing grip slip.

- **One-finger forehand grip** – Only the index finger is placed along the rim, sacrificing power for improved touch and finesse on short forehand shots.

D. Specialized Grips for Overhand Throws

Overhand throws, such as thumbers and tomahawks, require modified grips that allow for clean vertical releases. These grips help generate height and forward penetration, making them useful for navigating tight fairways, clearing obstacles, or executing trick shots. Proper hand positioning ensures the disc travels as intended and does not slip upon release.

- **Thumber grip** – The thumb is placed on the inside rim, while fingers grip the outer edge, creating a steep flight path that flips end over end.
- **Tomahawk grip** – The index and middle fingers grip the inside rim, with the thumb securing the top of the disc. This grip allows for controlled flight patterns that cut through obstacles.

E. How to Refine Your Grip for Maximum Performance

A strong grip directly translates to better shot execution. Players can refine their grip technique through deliberate practice and adjustments. Small refinements in grip pressure, finger positioning, and release mechanics can lead to more consistent throws. Developing a feel for the right grip ensures smoother releases and prevents common mistakes that lead to errant shots.

- **Experiment with different grips** – Testing various grips helps determine which feels most natural and effective for different shot types.
- **Focus on a smooth release** – A clean grip reduces flutter and ensures the disc follows the intended flight path.
- **Adjust for weather conditions** – Wet or humid conditions can affect grip consistency, so using towels, grip bags, or adjusting pressure can help maintain control.

- **Find the right grip pressure** – A balance between firm control and a relaxed grip prevents common mistakes such as early releases or grip lock.

F. Key Takeaways

Grip is the foundation of every throw in disc golf, directly influencing accuracy, control, and consistency.

- **Backhand grips** – The power grip is best for distance, while the fan grip improves accuracy and touch for approaches and putts.

- **Forehand grips** – The two-finger grip provides the most stability and snap, while the stacked grip increases control.

- **Overhand grips** – The thumber and tomahawk grips allow for unique vertical throws that help navigate obstacles.

- **Grip mechanics** – Proper finger placement, thumb pressure, and grip tightness help prevent early releases and inconsistent shots.

- **Refining grip technique** – Practicing different grips, adjusting pressure, and ensuring smooth releases contribute to better overall performance.

By developing a strong, consistent grip, players can improve their ability to execute precise and powerful throws across all shot types. The next section explores the backhand throw, breaking down power generation, accuracy, and proper release points.

4.2 Backhand Throw: Power, Accuracy & Release Points

The backhand throw is one of the most versatile and widely used techniques in disc golf. It allows players to generate power, accuracy, and control, making it essential for long-distance drives, controlled approach shots, and precise putting. Mastering the backhand throw requires refining grip, body mechanics, and release angles to maximize both distance and precision. Whether executing a controlled approach shot or a full-power drive, understanding the key elements of the backhand throw helps players develop consistency and confidence on the course.

The backhand throw is the foundation of disc golf—master it for maximum distance and accuracy.

A. The Mechanics of a Proper Backhand Throw

A successful backhand throw depends on a combination of grip, stance, weight transfer, and follow-through. These mechanics work together to generate power while maintaining accuracy and control. A well-executed backhand throw ensures a clean release, allowing the disc to fly smoothly without unnecessary wobble or instability.

- **Grip** – A secure grip is essential for a clean release and controlled spin. Most players use a power grip for long-distance shots and a fan grip for more controlled approach shots.

- **Stance** – A solid, balanced stance provides the foundation for power generation. The knees should be slightly bent, and the feet should be shoulder-width apart, with the body perpendicular to the target.

- **Weight transfer** – Power in a backhand throw is generated by shifting weight from the back foot to the front foot. This motion adds momentum and increases throwing distance.

- **Arm pull-through** – The arm should be pulled back before extending forward in a straight, level plane. Keeping the disc close to the body during the pull-through helps maintain speed and control.

- **Follow-through** – A complete follow-through ensures a smooth release. After the disc is released, the arm should continue its natural motion, and the back foot may pivot to maintain balance.

B. Generating Power & Distance

Generating power and distance is one of the key advantages of the backhand throw. By utilizing proper footwork, body rotation, and wrist snap, players can maximize distance without sacrificing control. A proper combination of these elements leads to an efficient throw, allowing for greater shot consistency and accuracy.

- **X-step footwork** – The X-step is a technique used to build momentum, where the back foot crosses over the front foot before the throw. This movement increases hip rotation and adds power to the throw.

- **Hip and shoulder rotation** – Engaging the hips and shoulders during the throw is essential for generating rotational force. As the hips rotate, the shoulders follow, storing energy that is released into the disc upon release.

- **Snap and wrist acceleration** – A wrist snap adds spin and stability to the disc. A strong snap accelerates the disc and helps maintain its flight path. Timing the snap properly ensures a clean release and maximum power.

- **Proper timing** – Coordinating the timing of the throw is essential for power generation. The arms, hips, and legs must work together in sync to generate optimal speed.

C. Achieving Accuracy & Control

While generating power is important, accuracy ensures that the backhand throw lands where it is intended. Controlling release angles and adjusting for various situations is key to executing precise backhand shots. Players who develop consistent accuracy can navigate tight fairways, land approach shots within putting range, and avoid unnecessary strokes caused by errant throws.

- **Flat release** – A flat release helps keep the disc stable, ensuring it flies straight. This is ideal for straight shots and controlled approach shots.

- **Hyzer angle** – A hyzer release occurs when the disc is tilted slightly downward. For right-handed backhand throwers (RHBH), this causes the disc to curve left.

- **Anhyzer angle** – An anhyzer release occurs when the disc is tilted slightly upward. For RHBH players, this results in a right-turning flight path.

- **Grip pressure** – Grip pressure plays a significant role in accuracy. Too much pressure can lead to unwanted wrist roll, while too little can cause the disc to wobble.

D. Common Mistakes & How to Fix Them

Even experienced players can struggle with common mistakes in their backhand throws. Recognizing and correcting these mistakes is essential for improving consistency and overall performance. Identifying the root cause of errors allows players to make targeted adjustments, leading to better form and increased throwing confidence.

- **Rounding** – Rounding occurs when the throwing arm drifts too far from the body during the pull-through, resulting in a wide and inefficient throw. Keeping the disc close to the body and maintaining a straight line during the pull-through helps fix this issue.

- **Early release** – Releasing the disc too early results in weak throws that lack distance and control. A full pull-through ensures a clean release and better timing.

- **Grip lock** – Grip lock occurs when the player holds onto the disc too tightly, causing a late, erratic release. Finding the right balance in grip pressure prevents this issue.

- **Lack of follow-through** – Failing to complete the follow-through results in weak or off-target throws. Focusing on completing the entire throwing motion improves control over the disc.

E. Key Takeaways

The backhand throw is a key skill in disc golf, providing the foundation for most shots on the course. Mastering this technique allows players to execute a wide range of shots with confidence and precision. A strong understanding of grip, mechanics, power generation, and release control leads to more consistent and effective throws.

- **Grip** – The power grip and fan grip are essential for controlling spin and accuracy during backhand throws.

- **Body mechanics** – Proper stance, weight transfer, and arm pull-through contribute to generating power and maintaining control.

- **Release angles** – Flat, hyzer, and anhyzer releases allow players to shape their throws for different course conditions.

- **Common mistakes** – Rounding, early release, grip lock, and lack of follow-through can be corrected with focused practice and proper technique.

By refining the backhand throw, players can improve their consistency, distance, and accuracy, allowing them to perform better on any course. The next section will focus on the forehand (flick) throw, detailing when and how to use it effectively for different situations on the course.

4.3 Forehand (Flick) Throw: When & How to Use It

The forehand throw, commonly called the "flick," is an essential technique in disc golf that allows players to shape shots with precision and control. It provides a reliable alternative to the backhand throw, especially in situations where a right-curving shot (for right-handed players) is required. Mastering the forehand can help players navigate tight fairways, execute powerful skip shots, and handle windy conditions effectively. Because the forehand relies more on wrist speed and snap than full-body motion, proper technique is crucial for generating power while maintaining accuracy. This section explores the mechanics of the forehand throw, when to use it on the course, and how to correct common mistakes for maximum efficiency.

A well-executed forehand throw is perfect for shaping lines and handling tricky fairways.

A. Mechanics of a Proper Forehand Throw

A successful forehand throw depends on proper grip, stance, wrist snap, and follow-through. Unlike the backhand, which uses a longer reach-back motion, the forehand relies on a compact throwing motion with an emphasis on wrist action. Mastering these mechanics ensures a smooth, powerful, and controlled release.

- **Grip** – The most common grip for forehand throws is the two-finger grip, where the index and middle fingers press against the underside of the disc while the thumb rests on top for stability. Some players prefer a stacked grip, where the index finger is placed on top of the middle finger for added control.

- **Stance & Positioning** – A forehand stance is more open than a backhand stance, with the lead foot slightly pointed toward the target. A balanced stance ensures proper weight transfer and helps generate smooth, controlled power.

- **Wrist Snap** – The forehand throw relies heavily on wrist snap to generate spin. A quick flick of the wrist at release accelerates the disc, providing both power and stability. A strong wrist snap is essential for maintaining accuracy and minimizing wobble.

- **Follow-through** – A complete follow-through ensures a clean, controlled release. The throwing arm should continue its natural motion toward the target after release to maximize accuracy and prevent off-angle flights.

B. When to Use a Forehand Throw

The forehand throw is a valuable tool in a variety of disc golf situations, offering unique advantages that complement a player's overall shot selection. Knowing when to use the forehand allows players to develop a more complete game.

- **Right-Curving Shots** – For right-handed players (RHFH), the forehand naturally curves to the right, making it ideal for executing dogleg-right fairways and throwing around obstacles.

- **Tight Wooded Fairways** – The compact throwing motion of the forehand allows for precise, controlled throws in narrow fairways. This makes it especially useful for threading the disc through small gaps in densely wooded courses.

- **Skip Shots** – When thrown low and at an angle, forehand shots can skip off hard surfaces to gain additional distance or improve positioning.

- **Windy Conditions** – The forehand's lower release point and natural spin help keep the disc stable in headwinds.

- **Utility & Recovery Shots** – The forehand throw is a great tool for scrambling and recovering from difficult lies.

C. Common Mistakes & How to Fix Them

Many players struggle with the forehand throw due to improper mechanics, grip issues, or a lack of wrist snap. Identifying and correcting these common mistakes leads to more consistent and reliable forehand shots.

- **Off-Axis Torque (Wobble)** – A wobbly release is often caused by poor wrist snap or an inconsistent grip. To fix this, focus on firming up the grip and ensuring the wrist snap is quick and clean at release.

- **Over-Reliance on Arm Strength** – Many players mistakenly try to generate power using only their arm strength. Instead, focus on generating power through wrist snap, body rotation, and proper timing.

- **Grip Inconsistency** – A grip that is too loose results in inaccurate releases, while a grip that is too tight restricts wrist movement.

- **Rolling the Wrist** – Allowing the wrist to roll over too much during release can cause the disc to turn over or dive unpredictably.

- **Overthrowing** – Trying to force the disc too hard often results in loss of accuracy and control. Players should focus on a smooth, fluid throwing motion rather than relying on excessive force.

D. How to Improve Forehand Technique

Developing a consistent and powerful forehand throw requires practice and attention to detail. By focusing on mechanics and refining technique, players can improve their accuracy and reliability in forehand shots.

- **Work on Wrist Snap** – The forehand throw depends on a quick, controlled wrist flick. Practicing short flick shots with putters and midranges helps develop a smooth, repeatable wrist snap.

- **Use Overstable Discs for Control** – Overstable discs resist turning over and help maintain a predictable flight path.

- **Focus on a Clean Release** – A smooth release reduces wobble and keeps the disc on its intended flight path.

- **Drill with Standstill Throws** – Practicing forehand throws from a standstill position helps isolate form issues and build muscle memory for proper mechanics.

- **Analyze Throwing Motion** – Recording and reviewing throwing form can help players identify inconsistencies.

E. Key Takeaways

The forehand throw is an essential shot that provides players with more versatility and control in their game. Mastering the forehand adds an extra dimension to shot selection and course strategy.

- **Grip** – The two-finger grip is the most effective for stability and control.

- **Power Generation** – Power comes primarily from wrist snap, body rotation, and timing rather than arm strength.

- **Situational Use** – Forehand throws excel in right-curving shots, tight fairways, skip shots, and windy conditions.

- **Common Mistakes** – Wobbly releases, over-reliance on arm strength, inconsistent grips, and rolling the wrist can be corrected with focused practice.

- **Technique Refinement** – Improving wrist snap, using the right disc stability, and focusing on a clean release lead to more consistent and powerful forehand throws.

By developing a reliable forehand throw, players can expand their shot options and improve their overall performance on the course. The next section will focus on overhand throws, such as thumbers and tomahawks, and how to use these specialty throws effectively in different situations.

4.4 Overhand Throws: Thumbers & Tomahawks for Tactical Shots

Overhand throws, including thumbers and tomahawks, are specialized shots that provide unique flight paths and can be highly effective for navigating obstacles, tight fairways, and tricky course layouts. These throws utilize an overhead release, causing the disc to flip end-over-end, making them particularly useful for clearing trees, getting out of trouble, and executing precise vertical approaches. While not as commonly used as backhand or forehand shots, mastering overhand throws can add valuable versatility to a player's game, especially in challenging or confined situations. Players who develop strong overhand throws gain a strategic advantage when traditional shots are not viable, allowing for better recovery and course management.

Overhand throws like thumbers and tomahawks provide unique ways to escape tight situations.

A. Mechanics of Overhand Throws

Overhand throws require a specific combination of grip, arm motion, wrist control, and follow-through to execute effectively. Unlike backhand or forehand shots, these throws rely heavily on an overhead delivery, which influences the disc's rotation and trajectory. Proper mechanics ensure that the disc follows a predictable flight path, maximizing accuracy and control.

- **Grip** – The grip determines the spin and stability of the disc in flight. For thumbers, the thumb is placed inside the rim of the disc, with the fingers gripping the outer edge. For tomahawks, the index and middle fingers are positioned inside the rim, with the thumb resting on top. Ensuring a firm but comfortable grip prevents slipping and enhances release consistency.

- **Arm motion** – The throwing motion mimics that of a baseball or football throw, with a full overhead extension before the release. A smooth, controlled motion helps generate both power and accuracy, reducing the risk of erratic flight patterns.

- **Wrist snap** – A strong wrist snap adds spin and helps control the disc's flipping pattern. Without proper wrist engagement, the disc may wobble or veer unpredictably, making wrist snap a critical factor in throw effectiveness.

- **Follow-through** – Completing the full motion ensures that the throw remains smooth and balanced. The arm should continue its natural motion after release, and the body may pivot slightly to maintain stability and maximize throwing efficiency.

B. Thumber vs. Tomahawk: Key Differences

Thumbers and tomahawks share similarities in their execution but differ in grip orientation, flight characteristics, and ideal use cases. Understanding these differences allows players to determine which throw best suits their specific needs on the course.

- **Thumber** – The thumber grip, where the thumb is inside the rim and fingers grip the outer edge, causes the disc to rotate clockwise for right-handed throwers (RHBH). The typical flight path features a steep, over-the-top arc that finishes left. Thumbers are particularly useful for clearing obstacles and creating controlled landing zones.

- **Tomahawk** – The tomahawk grip, where the index and middle fingers are inside the rim and the thumb is on top, results in a counterclockwise rotation for RHBH players. The tomahawk follows a similar flipping pattern but typically finishes right, making it a preferred choice for longer overhand throws that need to cover more ground while maintaining accuracy.

C. When to Use Overhand Throws

Overhand throws shine in scenarios where traditional backhand or forehand throws may be difficult or impractical. Their unique flight paths allow players to navigate challenging course elements with greater ease.

- **Clearing obstacles** – When trees, bushes, or man-made structures obstruct a direct throwing path, overhand throws provide a way to throw over the obstacle rather than around it. The high-arcing flight allows players to avoid interference and land in more favorable positions.

- **Utility and escape shots** – When stuck in a difficult lie, such as behind thick foliage or inside a dense wooded area, overhand throws offer a quick escape. Their vertical launch angle helps players maneuver out of tight spaces without requiring a full throwing motion.

- **Quick vertical drops** – Overhand throws are particularly effective when players need the disc to drop quickly near the basket. The natural flipping motion of the disc causes it to stall in the air before descending rapidly, making it easier to land close to the target.

- **Wind control** – Wind can drastically affect disc flight, but overhand throws tend to be more resistant to unpredictable gusts. Since these throws cut through the air differently than backhand or forehand shots, they can be a reliable option in windy conditions.

D. *Common Mistakes & How to Fix Them*

Overhand throws require precise technique, and common errors can result in inconsistent or ineffective shots. Identifying and correcting these mistakes improves execution and reliability.

- **Incorrect grip** – A weak or improper grip leads to unstable flights and unpredictable landing zones. Ensuring that the grip is firm but not overly tight allows for clean releases and smoother flight patterns.

- **Overthrowing** – Excessive force often results in loss of control and erratic shot placement. Players should focus on a controlled, smooth throwing motion rather than relying solely on arm strength.

- **Poor angle control** – The angle of release is crucial in determining the disc's flight path. Releasing at too steep or too shallow an angle can cause excessive flipping, unwanted fades, or skips upon landing. Practicing various release angles helps improve shot consistency.

- **Lack of follow-through** – Cutting off the follow-through too early disrupts power transfer and affects accuracy. Completing the entire throwing motion ensures better control and reduces strain on the arm and shoulder.

E. *Key Takeaways*

Overhand throws are an essential tool for tackling obstacles, executing escape shots, and achieving controlled vertical drops. Mastering these throws enhances a player's ability to handle difficult situations and expand their shot selection.

- **Throwing mechanics** – Proper grip, arm motion, wrist snap, and follow-through contribute to the success of overhand shots.

- **Thumber vs. tomahawk** – The thumber finishes left, while the tomahawk finishes right, providing shot variety based on course layout and obstacles.

- **Strategic use** – Overhand throws excel in clearing obstacles, executing vertical drops, and navigating tight fairways where traditional shots are impractical.

- **Common mistakes** – Grip inconsistencies, excessive power, poor angle control, and lack of follow-through can be corrected with practice and refined technique.

By incorporating overhand throws into their skill set, players can navigate challenging course layouts more effectively and develop a well-rounded approach to shot execution. The next section will explore biomechanics and efficiency, focusing on maximizing power and consistency across all throwing techniques.

4.5 Biomechanics & Efficiency: Maximizing Power & Consistency

Maximizing power and consistency in disc golf requires more than just raw strength—it depends on efficient biomechanics, body coordination, and proper technique. The most effective players generate power through a combination of weight transfer, hip rotation, and timing rather than relying solely on arm speed. Understanding the principles of biomechanics helps players throw farther, reduce injury risk, and maintain accuracy across different shot types. By refining movement efficiency and eliminating unnecessary motions, players can develop a smoother, more controlled throwing technique that translates into greater consistency on the course. This section explores how body mechanics impact throwing efficiency and provides key strategies for improving power and consistency.

Efficient disc golf biomechanics improve power and consistency—focus on weight transfer and follow-through.

A. The Role of Biomechanics in Disc Golf

Disc golf is a full-body sport that requires efficient movement patterns to optimize performance while minimizing strain. The way a player moves through the throwing motion determines how much energy is transferred into the disc, affecting both power and accuracy. Mastering biomechanics helps players generate effortless distance while maintaining control over their shots.

- **Kinetic chain movement** – Power is generated from the ground up, beginning with the legs, transferring through the core, and finishing with the arm and wrist. Utilizing the entire body in a connected sequence ensures a smooth, powerful throw while reducing unnecessary strain on the arm.

- **Energy transfer** – Proper weight shift from the back foot to the front foot adds momentum to the throw. This controlled transfer allows players to maximize distance without relying solely on upper body strength, conserving energy for longer rounds.

- **Posture & balance** – Maintaining proper posture and balance throughout the throw helps improve accuracy and prevents the disc from veering off course. A strong, balanced stance creates a stable foundation for consistent mechanics and controlled releases.

- **Flexibility & mobility** – A flexible body allows for a greater range of motion, improving throwing mechanics. Increased mobility in the shoulders, hips, and core helps players generate more power and maintain fluid movement during their throws.

B. Generating Maximum Power

Throwing with power requires more than just arm speed—it involves full-body coordination, rotational force, and efficient energy transfer. Proper mechanics ensure that maximum power is generated while maintaining control over the disc's flight.

- **X-step technique** – The X-step is a crucial movement in backhand drives, where a crossover step builds momentum before the throw. This motion increases rotational force and helps engage the lower body to generate additional power.

- **Hip & shoulder rotation** – Engaging the hips and shoulders during the throw stores energy that is released when the arms extend forward. Proper rotation adds force to the throw, increasing both speed and distance without overexerting the arm.

- **Extension & follow-through** – Fully extending the throwing arm and continuing the motion after release ensures that maximum acceleration is applied to the disc. A strong follow-through helps maintain control, smoothness, and consistency in each shot.

- **Wrist snap & spin** – A well-timed wrist snap at release enhances disc spin, improving flight stability and accuracy. Increased spin helps keep the disc on its intended flight path, making it an essential component of powerful, precise throws.

C. Improving Throwing Efficiency

Throwing efficiency is about reducing wasted movement and ensuring that every motion contributes to power and accuracy. By refining their technique, players can throw with less effort while maintaining consistency across multiple rounds.

- **Smooth tempo** – Rushing a throw can lead to poor timing and reduced power. A fluid, controlled throwing motion improves timing, allowing for better acceleration and a more consistent release.

- **Compact pull-through** – Keeping the disc close to the body during the pull-through minimizes rounding, optimizing energy transfer. A compact motion enhances speed and control, leading to more predictable flights.

- **Proper release timing** – Releasing the disc at the right moment prevents early or late releases that can cause the disc to veer off course. Consistent release timing ensures better control over shot accuracy and distance.

- **Lower body engagement** – Utilizing the legs and core for power, rather than relying only on arm strength, produces effortless distance. Engaging the lower body allows for smoother, more efficient throws and reduces fatigue over long rounds.

D. Common Mistakes & How to Fix Them

Even experienced players can struggle with biomechanical inefficiencies that reduce power and consistency. Identifying and correcting these mistakes can lead to immediate improvements in throw mechanics.

- **Too much arm reliance** – Overusing the arm instead of engaging the full body results in reduced power and increased fatigue. Properly incorporating the legs and hips into the throw helps generate more distance with less strain.

- **Rounding** – When the arm swings outward instead of staying on a straight plane, it reduces efficiency and control. Keeping the disc close to the body during the pull-through prevents rounding and improves shot accuracy.

- **Overthrowing** – Attempting to force too much power into a throw can lead to loss of control and poor flight paths. Players should focus on smooth, efficient mechanics rather than muscling their shots.

- **Lack of follow-through** – Stopping the motion prematurely results in reduced power and inconsistent releases. A complete follow-through ensures maximum energy transfer and improves shot consistency.

E. Key Takeaways

Maximizing power and consistency in disc golf depends on efficient biomechanics, proper technique, and controlled movement. Understanding how the body works together during the throw allows players to generate more distance while reducing strain and fatigue.

- **Full-body coordination** – Power is generated through kinetic chain movement, utilizing the legs, core, and arm to create maximum force.

- **Proper mechanics** – Techniques like the X-step, hip rotation, wrist snap, and full follow-through all contribute to generating maximum distance and accuracy.

- **Throwing efficiency** – A smooth tempo, compact pull-through, and lower-body engagement optimize control and consistency throughout the throw.

- **Common mistakes** – Issues like relying too much on arm speed, rounding, and overthrowing can be corrected with proper technique and consistent practice.

By focusing on biomechanical efficiency, players can improve their throwing power, maintain consistency, and reduce the risk of injury. The next chapter shifts focus to the putting game, covering techniques for accuracy, consistency, and mental focus inside the circle and beyond.

Chapter 4 Review: The Fundamentals of Throwing

Chapter 4 explores the essential throwing techniques that form the foundation of disc golf. From mastering grip mechanics to refining backhand, forehand, and overhand throws, this chapter provides the key principles needed to develop power, accuracy, and consistency. Players learn how to maximize their throwing potential through efficient biomechanics, proper weight transfer, and a controlled release.

4.1 Proper Grip Techniques for Maximum Control

- **Finger placement & grip pressure** – A balanced grip promotes a clean, stable release with optimal spin.

- **Backhand grips** – The power grip generates maximum distance, while the fan grip enhances control for approaches and putts.

- **Forehand grips** – The two-finger grip offers stability and snap, while the stacked grip increases control for smoother releases.

- **Overhand grips** – The thumber and tomahawk grips produce distinct flight paths, ideal for navigating obstacles and tough course layouts.

4.2 Backhand Throw: Power, Accuracy & Release Points

- **Throwing mechanics** – Grip, stance, weight shift, and follow-through create a smooth and powerful backhand.

- **Generating power** – The X-step, hip rotation, and wrist snap work together to maximize throwing distance.

- **Controlling release angles** – Flat, hyzer, and anhyzer angles influence a disc's flight path for different shot needs.

- **Avoiding common mistakes** – Issues like rounding, early release, and grip lock can be corrected through proper form and repetition.

4.3 Forehand (Flick) Throw: When & How to Use It

- **Proper technique** – Wrist snap and grip stability ensure smooth, controlled forehand throws.

- **Best use cases** – Ideal for right-curving shots (RHFH), tight wooded fairways, skip shots, and wind-resistant throws.

- **Fixing common issues** – Addressing wobbling releases, over-reliance on arm strength, and grip inconsistencies improves accuracy.

4.4 Overhand Throws: Thumbers & Tomahawks for Tactical Shots

- **Throwing mechanics** – A strong grip, wrist snap, and overhead release create controlled flipping motion.

- **Thumber vs. tomahawk** – The thumber typically fades left (RHFH), while the tomahawk fades right, offering different shot shapes.

- **Situational advantages** – Useful for clearing obstacles, executing vertical drops, and making recovery shots from difficult lies.

4.5 Biomechanics & Efficiency: Maximizing Power & Consistency

- **Kinetic chain movement** – Proper weight transfer, hip rotation, and wrist snap generate effortless power and accuracy.

- **Throwing efficiency** – A smooth tempo, compact pull-through, and engaged lower body optimize consistency.

- **Avoiding bad habits** – Over-reliance on arm strength, rounding, and overthrowing can be corrected with proper mechanics and repetition.

Chapter 4 builds a strong foundation for improving both power and accuracy. Players who refine their grip, throwing form, and biomechanics will gain better control over their game. The next chapter focuses on putting, covering techniques and mental strategies to develop consistency and confidence on the green.

Chapter 5: Perfecting Your Putting Game

Putting is one of the most crucial skills in disc golf, often determining success in competitive play. A strong putting game requires technique, consistency, and mental focus. This chapter explores the two primary putting styles—spin putting and push putting—along with their advantages and best uses. Players will learn key stances and techniques that improve stability and accuracy, helping them adapt to different distances and conditions. The mental aspect of putting is also covered, focusing on routines, concentration, and staying composed under pressure. By refining these fundamentals, players can gain confidence, sink more putts, and lower their scores.

A strong putting game separates top players from the rest—practice your routine and refine your technique.

5.1 The Art of Putting: Spin vs. Push Putting Styles

Putting is a critical skill in disc golf, often determining the outcome of a round. While every player develops their own unique putting style, the two primary techniques used are spin putting and push putting. Both have their advantages and disadvantages, depending on the player's preferences, strengths, and the conditions of the course.

Finding the right putting style helps players improve accuracy, build confidence, and remain consistent under pressure. Understanding the differences between these styles and knowing when to use them can give players an edge on the green, leading to more made putts and fewer frustrating misses. This section breaks down each putting style, offering insights into grip, mechanics, and the best use cases for each method.

Spin or push putt? Find the style that suits your form and helps you sink more putts.

A. Spin Putting

Spin putting relies on generating high spin through wrist action, which helps keep the disc stable in flight and resist environmental factors such as wind. This technique is favored by players who prefer a more aggressive putting style, as it offers greater range and a direct line to the basket.

- **Mechanics** – Spin putts involve a firm grip and a strong wrist snap upon release to generate spin. The disc is typically held at an angle, and the wrist flick at release adds rotation, ensuring a straight and stable flight. A clean release is essential to minimize wobble and keep the putt on target. Players using this style must focus on wrist control to maintain accuracy.

- **Grip** – A power grip or modified power grip is commonly used, with fingers tucked underneath the rim for a firm hold. The thumb applies pressure on top to keep the disc steady before release. A secure grip enhances spin generation, though too much pressure can lead to inconsistent releases.

- **Advantages** – Spin putting is highly effective for long-range putts and windy conditions since the spin provides stability and a more predictable flight path. The extra speed and direct line to the basket also reduce the impact of outside factors such as wind gusts. Additionally, spin putts are less likely to drop too soon, making them useful for players who struggle with putts falling short.

- **Disadvantages** – This style requires precise wrist control and can be challenging for beginners to master. The added spin can cause putts to bounce off the chains if the angle is off, leading to more missed opportunities. Additionally, spin putting can be difficult to control for short putts, as the added force may cause overshooting.

B. Push Putting

Push putting is a more controlled, arm-driven technique that minimizes wrist action and relies on a straight-line motion toward the basket. This method prioritizes accuracy and consistency, making it a reliable choice for short to mid-range putts.

- **Mechanics** – Push putts are executed with a controlled, forward motion using the arm and shoulder, with minimal wrist movement. The disc is "pushed" toward the basket rather than spun, resulting in a softer flight that drops more naturally into the chains. A proper follow-through ensures that the disc stays on its intended line without veering off course.

- **Grip** – A fan grip or modified fan grip is commonly used, where the fingers are spread across the underside of the disc to provide stability. The thumb rests on top to maintain control. This grip allows for a smooth release, reducing the risk of wobbling or unpredictable flight patterns.

- **Advantages** – Push putting is highly effective for short putts because it minimizes errors caused by excessive spin or wrist movement. The controlled motion leads to consistent, repeatable results, making it easier to develop a reliable putting stroke. Additionally, push putting reduces the likelihood of putts bouncing off the chains, as it generally has a softer impact.

- **Disadvantages** – Push putting lacks the distance and wind resistance of spin putting, making it less effective for long putts. The lack of spin means the disc is more susceptible to air disturbances, and players may struggle with putts outside the circle. Additionally, players who rely solely on push putting may find it harder to adjust in high-pressure situations requiring more speed or angle control.

C. Which Style is Right for You?

Choosing between spin and push putting depends on personal preference, skill level, and course conditions. Both styles are effective when used correctly, and many professional players incorporate elements of both techniques to maximize their performance.

- **Spin putting** – Ideal for players who need extra range and prefer an aggressive, direct flight path to the basket. It is also a good choice for windy conditions, as the additional spin provides more stability.

- **Push putting** – Best suited for short putts and players who value consistency over distance. It requires less effort to control and offers a reliable way to make putts inside the circle.

- **Hybrid approach** – Some players blend both styles, using spin putting for long putts and push putting for short-range consistency. Experimenting with both techniques can help players develop a well-rounded putting game.

D. Key Takeaways

Both spin and push putting offer unique advantages and can be highly effective, depending on the situation and the player's individual strengths. Developing a solid putting style improves confidence on the green and helps players lower their scores.

- **Spin putting** – Generates high spin for long-range accuracy but requires precise wrist control and can lead to missed putts if not executed correctly.

- **Push putting** – Relies on a controlled arm motion, making it ideal for short putts and consistency but lacks the power needed for long-range putts.

- **Situational awareness** – Wind conditions, terrain, and basket positioning influence which putting technique will be most effective in any given scenario.

- **Versatility matters** – Mastering both styles allows players to adapt to different situations and improve overall consistency in putting performance.

By understanding both putting styles and developing proficiency in each, players can create a well-rounded putting game that suits any situation. The next section will explore putting stances and techniques to help improve stability and accuracy on the green.

5.2 Putting Stances & Techniques for Stability & Accuracy

The way you position your body while putting has a significant impact on your stability, accuracy, and consistency. A proper putting stance helps create a solid foundation for a smooth, controlled putt. By focusing on body alignment, balance, and posture, players can reduce the chances of wobbly or missed putts. The right stance can help players maintain control in different course conditions, from wind to uneven terrain. This section explores the various putting stances and techniques that enhance stability and improve accuracy, from fundamental approaches to advanced adjustments.

Stability and balance are essential for a confident and consistent putting stroke.

A. Key Elements of a Solid Putting Stance

Your stance serves as the foundation for the rest of the putt, influencing balance, alignment, and consistency. A stable stance ensures the putter moves in a controlled and repeatable motion, helping maintain a straight flight path toward the target. Without proper balance, even the best mechanics can be disrupted, leading to missed putts. Developing a stance that promotes stability and control is essential for consistent success.

- **Feet position** – Your feet should be shoulder-width apart to create a solid base. The toes should point toward the target, and weight should be evenly distributed. For longer putts, widening the stance can improve balance and help maintain stability.

- **Knee bend** – A slight knee bend allows for a fluid, controlled motion. Keeping the knees relaxed ensures smoother weight transfer and a more natural putting stroke. Too much bend can create instability, while too little may restrict follow-through.

- **Weight distribution** – Shifting weight slightly toward the front foot improves stability and ensures a controlled forward motion. Proper weight distribution prevents unnecessary movement and enhances consistency.

- **Upper body alignment** – The shoulders, hips, and feet should be in alignment to create a straight and repeatable putting stroke. Keeping a stable upper body reduces unnecessary movement that could interfere with accuracy.

- **Grip and wrist position** – A firm but relaxed grip keeps the putter steady and prevents unwanted wobbling. The wrist should remain stable throughout the motion, ensuring a smooth and controlled release.

B. Common Stances for Different Putting Distances

Selecting the right stance can improve comfort, balance, and accuracy based on the distance and angle of the putt. Each stance offers unique advantages, and players should experiment to find what works best for different putting scenarios.

- **Straddle stance** – This stance involves spreading the feet wider than shoulder-width, creating a low center of gravity for increased stability. It is particularly useful for longer putts and situations where obstacles require a modified stance. The straddle stance also helps maintain balance when putting from uneven terrain.

- **Square stance** – A straightforward stance where both feet are aligned directly with the target, providing a stable and repeatable motion. It is the most commonly used stance, particularly for short-range putts, as it simplifies alignment and follow-through.

- **One-step stance** – Players use a small step forward with the back foot to generate additional momentum. This stance is effective for medium-range putts where extra power is needed while maintaining control.

- **Staggered stance** – One foot is positioned slightly ahead of the other, allowing for a natural weight shift and improved balance. The staggered stance can help with accuracy and smooth execution, particularly for players who incorporate a slight forward motion in their putt.

C. Proper Techniques for Accurate Putting

In addition to stance, refining putting mechanics ensures accuracy and consistency across different distances and conditions. A controlled, repeatable technique helps minimize variables and increases the likelihood of making putts under pressure.

- **Smooth, controlled motion** – A putting stroke should be fluid, avoiding sudden or jerky movements. Players should focus on keeping the arm motion steady and repeatable.

- **Follow-through** – The arm should continue its natural motion toward the basket after release. A complete follow-through improves accuracy by keeping the putt on a straight line and reducing premature disc fade.

- **Consistent release** – Letting go of the disc at the same release point each time helps build muscle memory and improves putting accuracy. A clean, consistent release minimizes wobble and promotes a smooth flight.

- **Disc angle** – The release angle should be slightly hyzer or flat for right-handed players (RHBH), depending on the putting style and conditions. A consistent angle prevents the disc from drifting unpredictably.

- **Eye focus** – Keeping the eyes locked on a specific link in the chains or a target point on the basket helps improve accuracy. Maintaining visual focus throughout the motion enhances concentration and consistency.

D. Advanced Techniques for Stability & Consistency

Beyond basic techniques, experienced players can incorporate additional strategies to refine their putting and maintain accuracy in challenging situations.

- **Breathing & mental focus** – Controlled breathing helps calm nerves and improves focus during crucial putts. Taking a deep breath before a putt can create a sense of rhythm and confidence.

- **Pre-putt routine** – Establishing a consistent pre-putt routine, such as practice swings or visualization, improves focus and muscle memory. A structured routine enhances comfort and consistency.

- **Putting rhythm** – Developing a consistent rhythm prevents hesitation and ensures a fluid stroke. A smooth tempo reduces rushed or delayed releases, improving overall consistency.

- **Putting from the knees** – Kneeling putts help minimize movement and provide increased stability in certain situations, such as low-ceiling putts or windy conditions.

- **Using the wind to your advantage** – Adjusting putting technique based on wind direction can improve accuracy. Spin putts tend to be more resistant to wind, while push putts may require more adjustments. Learning how to read wind conditions and modify stance and release angles accordingly can prevent missed putts.

E. Key Takeaways

Stance and technique play a major role in putting consistency, influencing accuracy and confidence on the green.

- **Solid stance** – Proper foot placement, balance, and knee bend contribute to a stable and controlled putting motion.

- **Different stances** – Players can choose from the straddle, square, staggered, or one-step stance based on putting distance and comfort.

- **Smooth technique** – A fluid motion, consistent release, and proper follow-through are essential for improved accuracy.

- **Advanced adjustments** – Techniques such as breathing control, pre-putt routines, and wind adjustments enhance consistency.

- **Adapting to conditions** – Understanding environmental factors and how they affect putts ensures better course management.

By refining stance and putting mechanics, players can develop a more confident and effective putting routine. A well-practiced technique leads to improved accuracy and consistency, helping players succeed in various putting situations. The next section will focus on putting strategies for different distances, covering techniques for short-range, mid-range, and long putts.

5.3 Inside the Circle vs. Long-Range Putts: Adapting Your Shot

One of the key aspects of becoming a proficient disc golfer is mastering the ability to putt from both short and long distances. While the fundamental mechanics of putting remain consistent, the techniques and strategies used for putting inside the circle (within 10 meters of the basket) differ from those needed for long-range putts. Short-range putts demand precision and consistency, while longer putts require additional power, control, and adaptability. Players who can adjust their approach based on putting distance will have an advantage on the green, reducing missed opportunities and maintaining a more consistent score. This section focuses on refining putting techniques at various distances to help players improve their short and long-range accuracy.

Adjust your putting technique based on distance—finesse for short putts, power for long-range shots.

A. Putting Inside the Circle (10 Meters or Less)

Inside-the-circle putts are the most frequent and essential shots in disc golf. A strong putting game from this range builds confidence and ensures that players capitalize on scoring opportunities. These putts require consistency, proper mechanics, and mental focus to avoid unnecessary mistakes.

- **Closer stance** – A square stance is typically used for short putts, with feet positioned shoulder-width apart for balance. Some players prefer a staggered stance with one foot slightly forward, helping maintain stability while generating a smooth, controlled motion. Finding a stance that feels comfortable and repeatable is key to consistency.

- **Speed & accuracy** – Short putts should focus on precision rather than power. The goal is to release the disc with just enough force to reach the chains while minimizing the risk of overshooting or bouncing out. Consistently hitting the center of the chains improves putting success.

- **Minimal follow-through** – Unlike long putts that require a full extension, short-range putts benefit from a more compact follow-through. Keeping movements controlled and efficient prevents overexertion and helps maintain a straight release.

- **Mental focus** – Even short putts can be missed if a player loses concentration. Establishing a strong pre-putt routine, visualizing the shot, and committing fully to the putt help maintain consistency under pressure.

B. Long-Range Putting (Beyond 10 Meters)

Long-range putting requires a different approach, as it introduces more variables, including power generation, disc selection, and environmental factors. Players must develop mechanics that enable them to putt effectively from greater distances while maintaining control over flight path and accuracy.

- **Straddle stance** – Many players prefer a wider straddle stance for long putts, as it provides more stability and allows for better weight distribution. A straddle stance also makes it easier to maintain balance when putting from uneven terrain or around obstacles.

- **Increased follow-through** – Long putts require a smooth and extended follow-through to generate additional power and control. A fluid motion through the release helps ensure the putt reaches the target with the proper trajectory.

- **Grip & spin** – Adding spin to a long putt stabilizes the disc's flight and prevents wobbling. Using a firmer grip and emphasizing wrist snap helps generate the necessary spin to maintain a straight and consistent putt.

- **Disc selection** – Overstable putters perform well for long putts because they resist turning over and handle wind better. However, players may also choose a putter with more glide to maximize distance while maintaining control. Experimenting with different discs can help determine the best option for long-range putting.

C. Adjusting for Wind & Weather Conditions

Weather conditions play a significant role in putting success, especially on long putts where wind has more time to influence the disc's flight. Players must adapt their techniques depending on the type of wind they encounter.

- **Headwinds** – Headwinds can lift the disc and cause it to stall or veer off course. To counter this, players may need to use a more overstable putter, throw with a lower release angle, or add more spin to keep the putt on a stable flight path.

- **Tailwinds** – Tailwinds push putts downward, often causing them to drop short of the basket. Players should use a softer release and possibly choose a putter with more glide to maintain lift and ensure the putt reaches the target.

- **Crosswinds** – Crosswinds affect the disc's stability and can make putts drift off target. Adjusting aim, release angle, and disc selection helps counteract crosswind effects, allowing for better accuracy in unpredictable conditions.

- **Rain & cold weather** – Wet or cold conditions can impact grip and release. Players should focus on maintaining a firm but relaxed grip, using a dry towel to keep hands and discs dry, and adjusting power to compensate for any reduced grip strength.

D. Improving Consistency at Different Distances

Developing a strong putting game at various distances requires focused practice and an understanding of how different techniques impact results. Players who dedicate time to refining their skills from multiple putting ranges will see noticeable improvements in consistency.

- **Practice circle putting** – Short putts should be practiced regularly to reinforce muscle memory and eliminate unnecessary movements. Repeating short putts from different angles inside the circle helps establish consistency.

- **Long-range drills** – Practicing putts from outside the circle improves mechanics and builds confidence. Players should experiment with different grips, stances, and throwing techniques to determine what works best for long-range accuracy.

- **Pressure-based drills** – Creating high-pressure practice scenarios, such as setting goals for consecutive successful putts, helps players develop mental resilience for real-game situations.

- **Understanding limits** – Recognizing personal putting range and making smart decisions during a round prevents unnecessary risks. If a putt is outside a player's confident range, laying up for an easier next shot may be the best option.

E. Key Takeaways

Short-range and long-range putting require different techniques, but both are crucial for success in disc golf. Players who develop strong fundamentals for both distances will have an advantage in scoring and overall performance.

- **Inside the circle** – Short putts focus on accuracy, stability, and a controlled release. Keeping the follow-through compact and maintaining mental focus improves consistency.

- **Long-range putting** – Longer putts require more power, an extended follow-through, and proper spin control. Using the right disc and stance helps maximize accuracy from outside the circle.

- **Adjust for conditions** – Wind and weather significantly impact putts. Adjusting release angles, power, and disc selection improves putting success in varying environmental conditions.

- **Practice builds confidence** – Dedicated practice at different distances, using a consistent pre-putt routine, and developing mental toughness all contribute to improved accuracy and success on the green.

By mastering techniques for both short and long-range putts, players can increase their confidence, versatility, and ability to handle any putting situation. The next chapter will explore mental focus and pre-putt routines, providing strategies to help players refine their mindset for consistently successful putting under pressure.

5.4 Mental Focus & Routine: How to Stay Consistent Under Pressure

Mental focus and a consistent routine are what separate the best putters from the rest of the field. Putting is not just a physical skill but also a mental game, requiring players to stay calm, focused, and confident, especially in high-pressure situations. A strong mental approach can mean the difference between sinking crucial putts and letting nerves interfere with performance. Developing a pre-putt routine, maintaining composure in the face of distractions, and cultivating mental resilience are key factors that contribute to long-term putting success. This section explores strategies for improving mental focus, handling pressure, and creating a repeatable routine that leads to greater confidence on the green. With practice and the right mindset, players can improve their ability to execute putts reliably in any situation.

Confidence and routine help you perform under pressure—stay focused and trust your form.

A. The Importance of Mental Focus in Putting

Mental focus plays a critical role in putting success. When a player loses concentration, even short putts can be missed. Elite players train their minds to stay focused and composed, allowing them to execute putts with confidence regardless of external conditions. The ability to maintain a strong mental game helps players overcome nerves, distractions, and self-doubt, making them more consistent on the green.

- **Staying calm under pressure** – Nerves can cause hesitation, rushed strokes, or missed putts. Learning to control emotions and remain composed in high-pressure situations leads to more consistent results. Techniques such as deep breathing and visualization help players maintain focus and avoid panic.

- **Trusting your mechanics** – Doubt can lead to last-second adjustments that disrupt a putt's rhythm. Players who trust their technique and rely on muscle memory perform better under pressure. Confidence in mechanics allows for a smoother and more fluid putting motion.

- **Concentration on the target** – Instead of thinking about the consequences of missing, players should focus entirely on the aiming point, such as the center of the chains. Narrowing focus helps eliminate distractions and improves precision. Keeping eyes locked on the target throughout the motion increases accuracy.

B. Developing a Pre-Putt Routine

A consistent pre-putt routine builds confidence and eliminates unnecessary variables. The best putters approach every putt with the same sequence of actions, reinforcing a sense of control and focus. A structured routine helps players settle into a rhythm, reducing stress and promoting consistency across different situations.

- **Visualize the putt** – Before stepping up, players should picture the disc's flight path and imagine it dropping into the basket. Visualization reinforces confidence and primes the body for execution.

- **Take deep breaths** – Controlled breathing calms nerves and relaxes muscles, allowing for a smoother stroke. A deep inhale and exhale before a putt can reset focus and reduce tension.

- **Set a target focus** – Identifying a specific chain link or point on the basket narrows attention and reduces distractions. Players who consistently aim at the same spot develop better accuracy.

- **Consistent setup** – Using the same stance, grip, and motion before every putt builds muscle memory. Repetition ensures that putts feel natural and automatic, regardless of the situation.

C. Handling Pressure & Remaining Confident

Handling pressure is one of the biggest challenges in putting. Whether playing in a tournament, competing against friends, or facing a personal milestone, maintaining confidence is key to success. Players who learn to embrace pressure instead of fearing it can improve their ability to sink important putts.

- **Positive self-talk** – Internal dialogue affects performance. Players should replace negative thoughts with constructive affirmations, such as "I've made this putt before" or "Stay smooth and confident." Maintaining a positive mental approach reinforces trust in one's ability.

- **Breaking the task into smaller steps** – Thinking too much about the result can create anxiety. Instead, focusing on each part of the process—grip, stance, and follow-through—keeps the mind engaged in execution.

- **Embrace mistakes** – Even the best players miss putts. Instead of dwelling on misses, players should analyze what went wrong, adjust, and move forward with a positive mindset.

- **Trust your instincts** – In high-pressure moments, second-guessing can lead to hesitation and misfires. Players should commit fully to their routine and trust their training.

D. Staying Consistent Over Time

Mental resilience is developed through experience and practice. By consistently applying mental strategies, players build confidence and adaptability, improving performance across different conditions. Mental training should be treated as an essential part of disc golf practice, just like physical technique.

- **Repetition and experience** – The more players putt under varying conditions and pressure situations, the better they become at handling nerves and distractions. Regular practice enhances confidence and ensures players can perform in any setting.

- **Mindfulness and presence** – Focusing on the present moment rather than past misses or future results keeps the mind clear. Being fully engaged in the process leads to more consistent execution.

- **Focus on the process** – Players should emphasize following their routine rather than worrying about making or missing a putt. This process-oriented approach reduces stress and leads to more reliable results.

- **Challenge yourself in practice** – Setting specific goals, such as making ten putts in a row from a certain distance, creates game-like pressure in practice and builds confidence for real rounds.

E. Key Takeaways

Mental focus and a consistent routine are crucial to putting success, especially in high-pressure situations. Players who develop strong mental habits can execute putts confidently, regardless of distractions or nerves.

- **Mental focus** – Staying calm, trusting mechanics, and narrowing focus on the target improve consistency under pressure.

- **Pre-putt routine** – Visualization, deep breathing, and a consistent setup create a structured, repeatable approach for every putt.

- **Handling pressure** – Positive self-talk, breaking the putt into small steps, and embracing mistakes help players stay confident.

- **Mental consistency** – Repetition, mindfulness, and focusing on the process rather than the outcome contribute to long-term improvement.

- **Confidence building** – Practicing under pressure and applying mental strategies enhance resilience and lead to more reliable putting performance.

By strengthening the mental side of their game and implementing a structured pre-putt routine, players can improve their putting accuracy and confidence, regardless of the situation. The next chapter explores course management and strategy, helping players take a more tactical approach to their overall game.

Chapter 5 Review: Perfecting Your Putting Game

Chapter 5 focuses on the essential aspects of putting, helping players develop the skills necessary to become consistent and confident putters. From learning different putting styles to mastering mental focus and routines, this chapter provides a comprehensive guide to improving your putting game. Understanding how to control spin, adjust stances, and maintain a steady mindset is key to sinking putts under pressure.

5.1 The Art of Putting: Spin vs. Push Putting Styles

- **Spin putting** – Relies on wrist snap and high spin for distance and stability, making it effective for longer putts and windy conditions.

- **Push putting** – A controlled, consistent technique that emphasizes arm movement over wrist flick, ideal for short-range putts.

- **Choosing the right style** – Spin putting is effective for long, powerful putts, while push putting excels in short-range, high-accuracy situations. Many players develop a hybrid approach depending on distance and conditions.

5.2 Putting Stances & Techniques for Stability & Accuracy

- **Stance fundamentals** – Feet positioning, knee bend, and weight distribution contribute to balance and control during the putt.

- **Adapting stances** – A square stance is ideal for short, controlled putts, while the straddle stance provides better balance for long-range putts or when putting around obstacles.

- **Follow-through & grip** – A smooth, controlled follow-through with proper grip pressure ensures accuracy and consistency. Maintaining a relaxed but firm grip prevents wobbling and off-target releases.

5.3 Inside the Circle vs. Long-Range Putts: Adapting Your Shot

- **Inside the circle** – Close-range putts require minimal motion, precise aim, and confidence in execution.

- **Long-range putting** – Requires increased power, a controlled wrist release, and a smooth follow-through to maintain accuracy.

- **Adjusting for wind** – Headwinds cause putts to lift, while tailwinds push them down, requiring angle adjustments for consistent results.

- **Spin vs. loft control** – Some players increase spin to fight wind resistance, while others use a lofted putt for better accuracy in tricky conditions.

5.4 Mental Focus & Routine: How to Stay Consistent Under Pressure

- **Developing a putting mindset** – Confidence, focus, and commitment to the shot are essential for success.

- **Pre-putt routine** – Visualization, deep breaths, and consistent setup reinforce muscle memory and improve performance.

- **Handling pressure** – Learning to stay composed during competitive rounds, using mental cues to remain confident under stressful conditions.

- **Repetition builds consistency** – A structured practice routine strengthens both muscle memory and mental resilience.

Chapter 5 emphasizes the importance of consistency in both technique and mental approach to putting. By refining their putting form, adapting to different distances, and maintaining focus, players can significantly improve their short game. The next chapter shifts focus to course management, teaching players how to analyze fairways, navigate hazards, and develop a strategic approach to tackling different course layouts and conditions.

Part 3: Elevating Your Disc Golf Game

This section focuses on the strategies and skills needed to take your game to the next level. Whether refining shot selection, improving physical conditioning, or mastering the mental game, these insights will help you grow as a player. You'll learn how to analyze courses, adjust strategies based on terrain and weather, and make smart decisions under pressure. Additionally, we'll cover training techniques that enhance strength, flexibility, and endurance—key factors in improving distance and control. Mental preparation is just as crucial, and this section explores ways to stay focused, confident, and resilient in high-stakes situations. By developing a well-rounded approach that includes strategy, fitness, and mindset, you'll gain the tools to excel in both casual play and competitive tournaments.

Chapter 6: Disc Golf Strategy & Course Management

Disc golf isn't just about throwing well—it's about making smart decisions that maximize performance and minimize mistakes. This chapter explores when to play aggressively versus when to take a safer approach, helping players navigate different situations with confidence. You'll learn how to analyze fairways, identify obstacles, and adjust shot selection based on course layout and conditions. Strategies for adapting to wind, rain, and other weather challenges are also covered to keep your game consistent. Finally, you'll discover how to execute recovery shots and scramble effectively when things don't go as planned. By mastering these strategies, players can improve decision-making, save strokes, and tackle any course with confidence.

Smart disc golf isn't just about throwing—it's about planning, adapting, and executing the right shots.

6.1 Shot Selection: When to Play Aggressive vs. Safe

Shot selection is one of the most important aspects of course management in disc golf. Knowing when to play aggressively or conservatively can significantly impact your score and overall strategy. While aggressive shots offer the potential for birdies or eagles, they also come with higher risks that can lead to bogeys or worse. On the other hand, safe shots provide consistency and minimize errors but may limit scoring opportunities. The key to successful shot selection is evaluating the situation, weighing the risks and rewards, and adapting your approach based on the course, conditions, and your confidence level. This section explores the key factors that influence shot selection and provides strategies for finding the right balance between aggression and safety in your game.

Knowing when to attack and when to lay up can make all the difference in your final score.

A. Understanding Aggressive Shot Selection

Aggressive shots aim to gain maximum distance, reach the green in fewer throws, or capitalize on scoring opportunities. These shots often involve challenging obstacles, tight landing zones, or high-risk plays that demand precise execution. While aggressive shots can provide game-changing advantages, they must be approached with confidence and an understanding of potential consequences.

- **When to go aggressive** – Aggressive shots are best when the risk is manageable, and the potential reward justifies the challenge. If you have a clear line to the target and the course layout favors your strengths, taking an aggressive approach can help gain strokes on the competition.

- **Shot types** – Common aggressive plays include attempting to drive the green on a shorter hole, going for long putts instead of laying up, or threading a shot through a narrow gap in the trees. Skilled players may use anhyzer or flex shots to shape lines around obstacles and maximize distance.

- **Risk assessment** – Before committing to an aggressive shot, consider the consequences of a missed execution. If a failed attempt results in an out-of-bounds penalty, a deep rough lie, or an unplayable position, it may not be worth the risk.

B. Understanding Safe Shot Selection

Safe shots focus on keeping the disc in play, minimizing errors, and avoiding high-risk situations. While they may not always set up ideal birdie chances, they prevent costly mistakes and allow for consistent scoring. Many players rely on safe shot selection to avoid unnecessary penalties and maintain control over their game.

- **When to play safe** – Safe shots are the preferred option when aggressive plays pose too much risk, such as when a hole has OB areas, water hazards, or dense woods that could lead to difficult recoveries. If you are leading a tournament or in a comfortable position on the leaderboard, playing safe can help protect your score.

- **Shot types** – Safe shots typically involve controlled midrange throws, placing the disc in wide landing zones, and laying up on longer putts instead of attempting a risky bid. Players may choose to throw putters or midranges instead of drivers to prioritize accuracy.

- **Risk mitigation** – Safe shots reduce the likelihood of bogeys and double bogeys. Even if a safe shot doesn't result in a birdie, it keeps the player in a favorable position for an easy par.

C. Key Factors in Choosing Aggressive vs. Safe Shots

Several factors influence whether an aggressive or safe shot is the best choice. Recognizing these factors during a round can help players make smarter strategic decisions and adjust their approach as needed.

- **Course layout** – Some courses reward aggressive play, while others punish it. Wide-open holes with forgiving fairways allow for more aggressive drives, while wooded courses with tight gaps often favor controlled, safe shots.

- **Weather conditions** – Wind, rain, and temperature affect shot selection. A strong headwind may turn an aggressive long-range shot into a risky play, while a tailwind can make aggressive throws more viable. Crosswinds require precise disc angles, making safe throws a smarter option in challenging conditions.

- **Player skill and confidence** – Understanding your strengths and weaknesses is crucial. If you are confident in your ability to execute a challenging shot, aggression may pay off. However, if you lack consistency in a specific type of throw, opting for a safer play is often the better decision.

- **Current score and game situation** – Your position in the round or tournament influences shot selection. If you need to catch up, calculated aggressive plays may be necessary to gain strokes. If you're leading, taking a safer approach can help maintain your advantage.

D. Combining Aggressive and Safe Shots for Strategic Play

The best players blend aggressive and safe shots to maximize scoring potential while minimizing risks. A strategic approach involves knowing when to push for an advantage and when to play conservatively.

- **Aggressive tee shots, safe approaches** – Some holes favor aggressive drives to gain an advantage off the tee while requiring a more controlled approach shot to avoid hazards. This balance allows players to capitalize on distance without jeopardizing their ability to secure an easy putt.

- **Playing hole-by-hole strategy** – Instead of committing to an entirely aggressive or safe round, players should analyze each hole individually. Some holes may require patience and controlled placement, while others offer opportunities to attack for birdies.

- **Adjusting to momentum and confidence** – If you are executing aggressive shots well, you may feel comfortable continuing to take calculated risks. If mistakes begin to pile up, it might be time to switch to a safer strategy to regain stability.

E. Key Takeaways

Successful shot selection requires the ability to assess risks, rewards, and situational factors on the course.

- **Aggressive shots** – High-risk, high-reward plays that offer scoring opportunities but require precision and confidence. Use them when conditions favor success.

- **Safe shots** – Controlled, low-risk plays that prioritize keeping the disc in play and avoiding penalties. These shots help maintain consistency and prevent mistakes.

- **Course and weather considerations** – Analyze the course layout and weather conditions to determine whether an aggressive or safe approach is optimal for each hole.

- **Strategic balance** – A well-rounded game plan includes a mix of aggressive and safe shots, allowing for flexibility based on performance and circumstances.

By mastering the balance between aggression and safety, players can navigate the course more effectively, reduce unnecessary mistakes, and maximize their scoring potential. The next section explores how to read a course, analyze obstacles, and navigate different types of terrain to enhance shot execution and overall performance.

6.2 Reading the Course: Analyzing Fairways, Obstacles & Elevation

One of the most important skills for any disc golfer is the ability to read the course effectively. Understanding how to analyze the layout of fairways, identify obstacles, and assess elevation changes allows players to make informed decisions about shot selection and strategy. The ability to navigate different course features can mean the difference between a well-executed round and a frustrating struggle with poor placement. Learning to read the course improves decision-making, minimizes unnecessary risks, and enhances overall consistency. This section explores key elements such as fairways, obstacles, and elevation, helping you develop a more tactical approach to your game.

Reading the course is just as important as executing the shot— analyze your surroundings before you throw.

A. Understanding Fairways and Landing Zones

The fairway is the primary path between the tee and the basket, and its design significantly influences how players approach each hole. By studying the fairway layout, players can anticipate where to place their shots, avoid trouble areas, and optimize their next move.

- **Straight vs. dogleg fairways** – Some fairways allow for direct shots, while others feature sharp turns (doglegs) requiring well-placed throws. Dogleg fairways often force players to plan their shots one step ahead, considering both their landing zone and the angle needed for the next throw. Understanding when to use a controlled hyzer, anhyzer, or flex shot can help navigate these layouts more efficiently.

- **Fairway width and difficulty** – Wide fairways offer more room for error, allowing players to choose a variety of lines to the basket. Narrow fairways, however, demand precision, as trees, bushes, or OB areas can punish errant throws. Recognizing when to play a high-power shot or when to prioritize control can improve consistency.

- **Strategic landing zones** – Identifying the best landing zones ensures that players set themselves up for an optimal next shot. Some holes may have obvious safe zones, while others require creativity in shot placement to avoid obstacles. By planning ahead and selecting controlled placement shots, players can avoid trouble areas and gain an advantage.

B. Analyzing Obstacles and Hazards

Obstacles are an inherent part of disc golf, and learning how to navigate them efficiently can give players a significant competitive edge. Recognizing obstacles early and adjusting shot selection accordingly can prevent unnecessary strokes.

- **Trees and tight gaps** – Trees create natural challenges that require players to shape their shots accordingly. When faced with a tight gap, disc selection and angle control become critical. Choosing a disc that naturally fades in the right direction or throwing a controlled forehand can help avoid collisions.

- **Water hazards and OB areas** – Water hazards add an element of risk to shot selection, forcing players to decide between a safe lay-up or an aggressive shot over water. Out-of-bounds (OB) areas—such as roads, fences, or artificial boundaries—require caution, as penalties can be costly. Players should evaluate whether the potential reward of an aggressive play outweighs the risk of landing OB.

- **Wind and weather conditions** – Environmental factors impact the flight path of a disc. Headwinds can push a disc off course, while tailwinds can cause it to overshoot the target.

Crosswinds demand adjustments in release angle and disc stability. Players who read wind conditions correctly can adapt their game and maintain control in adverse weather.

C. Accounting for Elevation Changes

Elevation plays a major role in shot execution, affecting both distance and accuracy. Understanding how to adjust for uphill, downhill, and sidehill lies will lead to better shot placement and improved consistency.

- **Uphill shots and added power** – Throwing uphill requires extra power and a higher release angle to counteract gravity. Discs tend to lose speed and stall more quickly on uphill shots, so players may need to choose a more overstable disc or adjust their throwing motion to achieve the desired distance.

- **Downhill shots and control** – Downhill shots add speed and glide to a disc's flight, often causing players to overthrow their target. To counteract this, using a more understable disc or adjusting the release angle to a flatter throw can prevent overshooting the landing zone.

- **Sidehill stances and adjustments** – Sidehill lies can make stance and balance challenging. When the disc is on a slope, players must adjust their footing and weight distribution to maintain control. Uphill stances typically require more power, while downhill stances may need a more compact, controlled motion to prevent loss of accuracy.

- **Reading elevation for shot strategy** – Certain course layouts feature dramatic elevation changes that require careful planning. Analyzing how elevation affects each throw allows players to select the best approach to maximize both distance and accuracy.

D. Course Strategy: Reading the Layout for Smarter Play

Players who actively analyze the course as they play will make smarter decisions and avoid unnecessary risks. Understanding how fairways, obstacles, and elevation work together allows for better strategic play.

- **Studying the course before playing** – Walking the course or reviewing hole maps can provide key insights into shot selection. Identifying tricky areas and planning alternative shot routes before a round can prevent mistakes during competition.

- **Adapting to course design** – Some courses favor specific playing styles. A heavily wooded course requires precision and controlled shots, while an open course may favor distance and aggressive drives. Knowing which aspects of your game to emphasize based on the course layout can help improve overall performance.

- **Recognizing common mistake areas** – Some holes have notorious trouble spots where players frequently lose strokes. Being aware of these areas and choosing a safe play when necessary can help avoid costly errors.

- **Making adjustments mid-round** – As conditions change, so should your approach. If a certain strategy isn't working, adapting to a safer or more aggressive style based on how the course is playing can lead to better results.

E. Key Takeaways

Understanding how to read a course and adjust shot selection based on layout, obstacles, and elevation is essential for strategic disc golf play.

- **Fairway navigation** – Recognizing the best landing zones and evaluating fairway width helps players shape their shots effectively and avoid unnecessary risks.

- **Obstacle management** – Trees, water hazards, and OB areas demand smart shot selection and adjustments in angle, power, and placement.

- **Elevation adjustments** – Uphill and downhill throws require different power and control strategies, and sidehill lies demand stance modifications to maintain accuracy.

- **Strategic course play** – Pre-round planning, adaptability, and recognizing high-risk areas contribute to smarter decision-making on the course.

By refining your ability to read a course and anticipate challenges, you can improve shot selection and develop a more tactical approach to your game. The next section will explore how to adjust your game for different weather conditions, ensuring you can adapt and maintain consistency in varying environments.

6.3 Playing Smart in Different Weather Conditions

Weather conditions play a major role in a disc golfer's performance and decision-making process. Wind, rain, and temperature changes can all influence how a disc behaves in flight, how difficult it is to maintain control, and how effectively you can execute shots. Understanding how to adjust your game and adapt to these conditions is key to maintaining consistency and minimizing mistakes. This section explores how various weather conditions affect disc golf play and provides strategies for playing smart, regardless of the weather.

Wind, rain, and temperature changes affect flight paths—adapt your game to the conditions.

A. Playing in Windy Conditions

Wind is one of the most challenging factors in disc golf, as it can drastically alter the flight path of your discs. Knowing how to adjust your shot selection and technique when the wind is blowing is essential for staying on track.

- **Headwind** – A headwind pushes against the disc, slowing it down and potentially causing it to drop prematurely. When putting into a headwind, you may need to use a more overstable disc and throw with more power to compensate for the wind resistance. On drives, it's advisable to throw a disc with a more stable flight path to reduce the risk of the disc turning over.

- **Tailwind** – A tailwind pushes the disc forward, potentially adding more distance than expected. However, it can also cause the disc to overshoot, especially on putts. When facing a tailwind, it's important to throw with less power and use a more understable disc to help maintain control and prevent overshooting the target.

- **Crosswind** – Crosswinds can push the disc off to the left or right, causing it to drift unexpectedly. In these conditions, players should focus on adjusting the angle of release and disc selection. For example, throwing a hyzer or anhyzer may be necessary to counteract the wind's push. Practicing these adjustments can help you stay on target despite the crosswind's effects.

B. Playing in the Rain

Rain can make a significant impact on both the physical aspects of the game and the disc itself. When playing in wet conditions, discs are more likely to absorb water, affecting their flight stability, grip, and distance. It's important to have a strategy for managing these factors to maintain control over your game.

- **Grip issues** – Wet discs are harder to grip, which can affect the consistency and accuracy of your shots. Keep a towel handy to dry your hands and discs between throws. If the rain is particularly heavy, consider using a wetter towel to wipe down the disc or changing to a more textured disc for better grip.

- **Disc stability** – In wet conditions, discs become heavier and more difficult to throw with the same precision. This can lead to a decrease in distance, particularly on drives. Consider using more overstable discs that will hold their line better in windy and rainy conditions.

- **Visibility and course conditions** – Rain can make it harder to see the target, particularly on long-range shots, and can cause the ground to become slippery. Pay attention to the terrain and avoid throwing risky shots on wet, muddy ground that could lead to slips or poor footing. Keep your body movements deliberate and your balance steady.

C. Playing in Hot or Cold Weather

Temperature extremes also influence performance. Hot weather can lead to fatigue and dehydration, while cold weather can make discs harder to grip and affect their flight. Here are a few tips for dealing with temperature-related challenges.

- **Hot weather** – Playing in the heat requires extra hydration and sun protection. Dehydration can affect your energy and concentration, so drink plenty of water throughout the round. Additionally, wearing breathable, moisture-wicking clothing helps to keep you cool and comfortable. Be mindful of heat exhaustion, which can impair performance and focus.

- **Cold weather** – In cold conditions, discs become stiffer and less responsive, especially in freezing temperatures. Be prepared for this by choosing more overstable discs, which are less affected by the cold. Wearing layers and keeping your hands warm will also help maintain control over the disc. If it's particularly cold, make sure to dry your hands frequently and keep your discs in a warm place when not in use to prevent them from becoming too stiff.

D. Strategies for Adapting to Different Weather Conditions

In addition to adjusting for specific weather conditions, it's important to approach the game with a flexible mindset and a focus on maintaining consistency. Here are strategies to keep in mind for all weather conditions:

- **Adjust your expectations** – When playing in difficult weather, adjust your expectations for distance and accuracy. Be willing to accept that your shots may not be as precise as usual, and focus on playing a more conservative, controlled game to reduce mistakes.

- **Plan for the weather** – Before a round, check the weather forecast and prepare accordingly. Dress appropriately, bring extra towels, and ensure your discs are ready for the conditions. Planning ahead will help you stay comfortable and focused throughout the round.

- **Adapt your strategy** – In windy or rainy conditions, consider playing more conservative shots, laying up short of hazards, and focusing on accuracy instead of distance. In extreme temperatures, adjust your pacing to ensure you don't tire out or become mentally fatigued.

E. Key Takeaways

Playing in varying weather conditions requires adaptability and smart decision-making.

- **Wind** – Adjust your shot selection based on wind direction, using overstable discs in headwinds and less power in tailwinds. Crosswinds require careful angle adjustments to maintain the disc's flight path.

- **Rain** – Keep your discs dry, maintain a strong grip, and choose overstable discs to compensate for weather-related changes. Pay attention to course conditions and visibility when it's wet.

- **Hot & cold weather** – Hydrate in hot weather, dress in layers in cold weather, and adjust for changes in disc stability and grip caused by temperature extremes.

- **Adapt your strategy** – Maintain flexibility in your strategy and adjust your expectations for distance and accuracy, focusing on controlled shots to minimize errors.

By understanding how different weather conditions affect disc flight and course play, players can adapt their techniques and strategies to perform at their best in any conditions. The next chapter will explore recovery shots and strategies for managing difficult situations, helping you save strokes when things don't go as planned.

6.4 Recovery Shots: Scrambling & Saving Strokes

In disc golf, things don't always go as planned. Whether you've landed in thick rough, hit a tree, or ended up in an out-of-bounds area, recovery shots are essential for minimizing damage and saving strokes. A strong scrambling game allows you to get back on track after an imperfect shot, keeping you in contention for a low score even when things go wrong. This section covers the strategies and techniques for executing effective recovery shots, including how to adapt your approach based on the course conditions and your lie. By developing your scrambling skills, you'll be able to turn difficult situations into opportunities to save strokes and improve your overall game.

Great disc golfers turn bad lies into great recoveries—develop your scrambling skills.

A. Understanding Scrambling

Scrambling is the art of recovering from an off-target shot and saving par or minimizing the damage to your score. It requires a combination of creativity, adaptability, and a solid understanding of your abilities to get out of trouble. Scrambling is not just about making up for a bad shot—it's about staying mentally focused, assessing the situation, and executing a smart shot that can get you back on track.

- **Mental approach** – The key to effective scrambling is staying calm and confident, even when things don't go as planned. A positive mindset allows you to focus on the task at hand and make smart decisions without letting frustration affect your performance.

- **Shot selection** – When scrambling, you must quickly assess your options. Choose the shot that gives you the best chance of getting back into a good position, rather than trying to force a risky, high-reward shot. Playing for position, rather than trying to gain distance, is often the wisest choice.

- **Adaptability** – Being able to adjust your shot selection based on your lie and the conditions around you is essential. Recovery shots often require creativity and thinking outside the box to navigate through trees, over obstacles, or around hazards.

B. Types of Recovery Shots

Depending on the situation, various recovery shots may be required. These shots typically focus on accuracy and placement over distance, as you need to get back into a favorable position for your next shot.

- **Layups** – Layups are safe, controlled shots designed to position the disc for an easy follow-up shot. They are useful when you've found yourself in an undesirable lie or near an OB area and need to minimize risk.

- **Forehand or Flick Recovery** – The forehand (or flick) throw is a useful recovery shot when you're facing a low ceiling or need to curve the disc around obstacles. The forehand is often more reliable than a backhand for tight spaces or awkward lies, providing better control.

- **Overhand Recovery (Thumber & Tomahawk)** – Overhand throws like the thumber and tomahawk are ideal for situations where you need to throw over obstacles or require a quick vertical drop. These shots are useful for navigating dense tree cover and difficult terrain.

- **Short-range putter shots** – A controlled putter shot can sometimes be the most effective recovery. Whether it's a short forehand, backhand, or an underhand toss, putter shots help with precision placement when getting out of trouble.

C. Playing for Position: Course Management During Scrambles

In a scramble situation, your primary goal should be getting back into a favorable position, not necessarily trying to make an aggressive play or go for the pin. Playing for position involves assessing the course layout, considering hazards, and placing your disc where you can make a more controlled shot on the next throw.

- **Choose your target** – Rather than aiming directly for the basket, aim for a spot that gives you the best angle or an open shot for your next throw. If you're in the rough, try to place the disc in a less obstructed area where you have a clearer path for your next shot.

- **Use your strengths** – Consider your strengths when selecting a recovery shot. If you're more comfortable with forehands, use that skill to navigate around obstacles. Similarly, if you're confident with your overhand throws, trust that shot to get you out of tight spots.

- **Stay aware of hazards** – Always be mindful of out-of-bounds areas, trees, and other obstacles when selecting a recovery shot. Play it safe by avoiding risky shots that could lead to a penalty stroke. Sometimes, laying up short of a hazard and leaving yourself a simple shot to the basket is the best decision.

D. Common Scrambling Mistakes and How to Avoid Them

While scrambling can be an effective way to save strokes, there are common mistakes that players make when trying to recover from tough situations. Recognizing these mistakes and correcting them can significantly improve your ability to recover and minimize mistakes.

- **Forcing difficult shots** – One of the most common scrambling mistakes is trying to force a risky shot that has a low chance of success. It's important to recognize when the odds are against you and take a safer route.

- **Rushing the shot** – When under pressure, players often rush their recovery shots, leading to poor execution. Take your time, set up properly, and focus on a controlled, accurate shot.

- **Not considering the next shot** – Another mistake is failing to think ahead when scrambling. It's easy to focus too much on getting out of the immediate situation, but you also need to consider how your recovery shot sets up the next throw.

E. Key Takeaways

Recovery shots are essential for minimizing mistakes and saving strokes, especially after errant throws or tricky lies.

- **Smart shot selection** – Play conservatively and focus on getting the disc back into a favorable position rather than going for risky, aggressive shots.

- **Types of recovery shots** – Use a variety of shots such as layups, forehands, overhand throws, or short-range putter shots based on the situation and obstacles.

- **Playing for position** – Prioritize positioning the disc for a better follow-up shot rather than forcing distance or accuracy.

- **Avoid common mistakes** – Avoid rushing shots, forcing difficult throws, or forgetting to consider the next shot.

- **Consistency under pressure** – Staying calm and sticking to a strategy is key for successfully scrambling and saving strokes.

By mastering recovery shots and adapting to challenging situations, players can minimize the damage from bad throws and keep their scorecards clean. The next chapter will focus on training and fitness, helping players enhance their physical performance and improve their disc golf game.

Chapter 6 Review: Disc Golf Strategy & Course Management

Chapter 6 explores the strategic side of disc golf, focusing on course management and decision-making. Knowing when to play aggressively or take a safer approach, how to read fairways and elevation changes, and how to adjust for weather conditions can significantly impact your overall performance. Additionally, this chapter highlights the importance of recovery shots, helping players save strokes and stay composed when faced with difficult situations.

6.1 Shot Selection: When to Play Aggressive vs. Safe

- **Aggressive shots** – High-risk, high-reward plays designed to maximize distance or set up birdie opportunities. These shots are ideal when obstacles are minimal, and conditions are favorable.

- **Safe shots** – More conservative plays that prioritize accuracy over distance, minimizing risk and keeping the disc in play. Safe shots are useful in tight fairways or high-penalty areas.

- **Finding the right balance** – Smart course management means knowing when to attack and when to play it safe. Making strategic decisions prevents unnecessary strokes and leads to more consistent scoring.

6.2 Reading the Course: Analyzing Fairways, Obstacles & Elevation

- **Fairway strategy** – Understanding fairway width, shape, and landing zones helps guide shot selection and disc choice. Players should aim for the most forgiving landing areas to set up easier approach shots.

- **Obstacle management** – Trees, water, and out-of-bounds areas influence decision-making. Identifying potential trouble spots before throwing can prevent unnecessary risks.

- **Elevation adjustments** – Uphill shots require more power and a higher release angle, while downhill shots need softer throws and controlled landings to prevent overshooting. Playing slopes strategically improves shot placement and consistency.

6.3 Playing Smart in Different Weather Conditions

- **Wind adjustments** – Headwinds require overstable discs, tailwinds call for controlled throws, and crosswinds demand precise angles to maintain stability.

- **Rain and grip control** – Wet conditions affect disc grip and stability, making towels and grip-enhancing techniques essential for maintaining consistency.

- **Temperature considerations** – Cold weather stiffens discs, reducing flexibility and grip, while heat softens them, affecting stability. Adjusting throwing power and disc selection accordingly ensures optimal performance.

6.4 Recovery Shots: Scrambling & Saving Strokes

- **Strategic scrambling** – Recovery shots focus on minimizing damage rather than forcing risky plays. Players should prioritize positioning over distance to set up an easier next throw.

- **Essential recovery throws** – Low approaches, controlled forehand flicks, and overhand shots like tomahawks and thumbers help escape trouble spots and get back into position.

- **Staying composed under pressure** – Maintaining confidence and making smart decisions in recovery situations can prevent a single mistake from turning into multiple lost strokes.

Chapter 6 provides the tools needed to make better strategic choices, manage obstacles, and adapt to different course conditions. The next chapter shifts focus to physical training, covering strength, endurance, and flexibility exercises to enhance performance and consistency on the course.

Chapter 7: Training, Fitness & Disc Golf Performance

Physical conditioning is essential for improving distance, accuracy, and consistency in disc golf. Strength, endurance, flexibility, and mobility all play a role in optimizing throws and preventing injuries. This chapter covers disc golf-specific workouts that build power, flexibility exercises that enhance range of motion, and strength training to improve distance and control. You'll also learn how to structure effective practice sessions to reinforce proper technique and maximize performance gains. By incorporating fitness into your routine, you'll increase stamina, reduce fatigue, and develop a more consistent throwing motion, giving you a competitive edge in every round.

A strong body leads to a stronger game—train smart to maximize your potential.

7.1 Disc Golf-Specific Workouts for Power & Endurance

Disc golf is a physically demanding sport that requires a balance of power, endurance, flexibility, and coordination. While the game may not seem as strenuous as traditional sports, it engages multiple muscle groups in explosive movements, requiring strength and stamina for optimal performance. Developing a structured workout routine focused on disc golf-specific exercises can help players improve their drives, maintain consistency throughout a round, and prevent injuries. This section outlines key workouts that enhance power, endurance, and mobility, allowing players to maximize their throwing potential and perform at their best. Whether you are looking to increase distance, improve accuracy, or build long-term stamina, these workouts provide the foundation needed to elevate your game.

Strengthen your body to increase power, endurance, and consistency in your throws.

A. Power Workouts for Disc Golf

Generating power in disc golf requires a combination of lower-body strength, core rotation, and upper-body coordination. By training for explosive movements, players can improve their throwing distance and maintain control over their shots.

- **Medicine Ball Slams** – This exercise builds explosive power in the core, shoulders, and arms, which are essential for strong, controlled throws. Hold a medicine ball overhead, engage the core, and slam the ball forcefully to the ground.

Perform 3 sets of 10-15 reps to increase strength and rotational power.

- **Kettlebell Swings** – Kettlebell swings focus on the hip hinge, an essential movement for generating power in a throw. Stand with feet shoulder-width apart, swing a kettlebell from between your legs to chest height, and repeat for 3 sets of 15-20 reps. This movement strengthens the lower back, hips, and core, which are crucial for maximizing drive distance.

- **Box Jumps** – Explosive lower-body strength contributes to stability and drive mechanics. Stand in front of a sturdy box, bend your knees, and jump onto the box, landing softly before stepping down. Complete 3 sets of 10 reps to build leg power and coordination.

B. Endurance Workouts for Disc Golf

Endurance is a crucial component of disc golf, as rounds often last several hours and require sustained energy levels. Building cardiovascular endurance and muscular stamina allows players to maintain peak performance from the first hole to the last.

- **Circuit Training** – A full-body circuit workout helps improve stamina and endurance. Include exercises such as burpees, lunges, push-ups, and mountain climbers in a sequence with minimal rest between sets. Complete 3-4 rounds with 30-second breaks to enhance both strength and endurance.

- **Running or Hiking** – Long rounds require significant walking, often over uneven terrain. Running and hiking build cardiovascular endurance while strengthening the legs and core. Aim for 30-45 minutes of steady-state cardio, incorporating hills to simulate the demands of disc golf courses.

- **Rowing or Cycling** – Both rowing and cycling provide low-impact cardiovascular conditioning while engaging the upper body. Perform steady-state rowing or cycling for 20-30 minutes to develop aerobic fitness without excessive strain on the joints.

C. Core Workouts for Stability & Power

The core is the powerhouse of disc golf mechanics, providing rotational force for throws and stability for controlled putting. Strengthening the core improves overall control, balance, and endurance.

- **Planks** – Planks build core stability, which is essential for a controlled throwing motion. Hold a plank position for 30-60 seconds, engaging the abs and back. Repeat for 3-4 sets, gradually increasing duration as strength improves.

- **Russian Twists** – This rotational exercise strengthens the obliques, which are heavily involved in throwing mechanics. Sit with knees bent, lean back slightly, and twist the torso while holding a weight. Perform 3 sets of 15-20 reps per side to enhance rotational strength.

- **Deadbugs** – This exercise improves core coordination and balance, helping players maintain control during throws. Lie on your back with arms extended upward and knees bent at 90 degrees. Lower one arm and the opposite leg toward the ground while keeping the core engaged. Complete 3 sets of 10-15 reps per side.

D. Flexibility and Mobility Work for Injury Prevention

Maintaining flexibility and mobility is essential for fluid movement and injury prevention. A greater range of motion in the shoulders, hips, and spine allows for smoother throws and reduces strain on muscles and joints.

- **Dynamic Stretching** – Warming up with dynamic stretches, such as arm circles, torso twists, and hip rotations, helps loosen muscles and prepare them for movement. Spend 5-10 minutes before a round or workout performing these active stretches.

- **Yoga** – Yoga improves flexibility, balance, and focus. Poses such as downward dog, pigeon pose, and seated spinal twists target key muscle groups used in disc golf. Practicing yoga regularly enhances mobility and reduces tightness that can lead to injury.

- **Foam Rolling** – Using a foam roller after rounds or workouts helps relieve muscle tightness and prevent soreness. Focus on rolling the quads, hamstrings, calves, and upper back, spending 10-15 minutes post-activity to aid recovery.

E. Recovery and Injury Prevention Strategies

Maintaining peak performance in disc golf requires proper recovery and injury prevention techniques. Neglecting recovery can lead to overuse injuries, fatigue, and decreased performance. Implementing effective recovery strategies ensures longevity in the sport.

- **Rest and Hydration** – Allowing the body to recover between workouts and rounds is essential for muscle repair and energy restoration. Staying hydrated throughout the day helps maintain muscle function and prevents cramps.

- **Proper Warm-ups and Cool-downs** – Always warm up before throwing or exercising to prevent muscle strain. A cool-down routine, including static stretching and foam rolling, helps the body transition to a resting state and prevents stiffness.

- **Strength Balance** – Ensuring that both sides of the body are equally trained prevents imbalances that can lead to injuries. Incorporate unilateral exercises such as single-leg deadlifts and one-arm kettlebell swings to improve muscle symmetry.

F. Key Takeaways

A well-rounded training program tailored to disc golf enhances power, endurance, flexibility, and mobility, leading to improved performance on the course.

- **Power Workouts** – Medicine ball slams, kettlebell swings, and box jumps help develop explosive strength for longer drives.

- **Endurance Workouts** – Circuit training, running, and cycling build the stamina necessary for long rounds and demanding courses.

- **Core Strength** – Planks, Russian twists, and deadbugs improve stability, control, and rotational power for throws.

- **Flexibility and Mobility** – Dynamic stretching, yoga, and foam rolling enhance range of motion and prevent injuries.

- **Recovery and Prevention** – Proper hydration, warm-ups, and strength balance exercises help maintain long-term performance and reduce injury risks.

By integrating these disc golf-specific workouts into your routine, you can develop the strength, endurance, and flexibility needed to elevate your game. The next chapter will cover structuring training sessions effectively, ensuring that every workout contributes to steady progress and peak performance.

7.2 Flexibility & Mobility Exercises for Better Throws

Flexibility and mobility are essential for achieving the range of motion needed to throw accurately and with power in disc golf. Tight muscles or limited joint mobility can restrict your throwing form, reduce power, and increase the risk of injury. By incorporating targeted flexibility and mobility exercises into your routine, you can improve your throwing mechanics, enhance overall performance, and stay injury-free on the course. A well-rounded flexibility and mobility program will help players maintain fluid movement, allowing for smoother, more controlled shots. This section highlights key flexibility and mobility exercises that will improve your throwing technique, helping you achieve better, more consistent throws.

Flexibility and mobility improve your throwing mechanics and help prevent injuries.

A. Importance of Flexibility & Mobility in Disc Golf

In disc golf, the throwing motion relies on the flexibility and mobility of various joints and muscle groups, particularly the shoulders, hips, back, and wrists. Limited flexibility or tightness in any of these areas can lead to poor form, reduced range of motion, and inefficient throws. Improving flexibility and mobility allows you to make the most of your body's natural movement patterns, helping you throw with more control, power, and precision.

- **Increased range of motion** – Greater flexibility in the shoulders, hips, and spine allows for more efficient rotations during the throwing motion, generating power while maintaining good form.

- **Improved body mechanics** – Proper flexibility and mobility enhance your ability to move freely through the throwing motion, allowing for smooth execution with less effort.

- **Injury prevention** – Flexibility helps reduce the risk of muscle strains, joint stiffness, and overuse injuries by keeping muscles and joints supple and able to handle the stresses of disc golf.

- **Better endurance and recovery** – Improved flexibility and mobility contribute to better movement efficiency, reducing fatigue and helping muscles recover faster after long rounds.

B. Key Flexibility Exercises for Disc Golf

Flexibility exercises focus on stretching and lengthening muscles to improve movement quality and throwing efficiency.

- **Shoulder Rotations** – Stand with arms extended to the sides, making small circles and gradually increasing their size. Perform for 30 seconds in each direction to loosen up shoulder muscles.

- **Thoracic Spine Twists** – Sit with legs extended, place one foot over the opposite knee, and twist toward the bent leg. Hold for 20-30 seconds per side to enhance spinal mobility.

- **Hamstring Stretch** – Stand with feet shoulder-width apart, bend at the hips, and reach for your toes. Hold for 20-30 seconds to improve flexibility in the hamstrings, aiding balance and stability.

- **Hip Flexor Stretch** – Kneel on one knee with the other leg bent at 90 degrees. Shift weight forward to stretch the hip flexors, holding for 20-30 seconds per side.

- **Wrist & Forearm Stretch** – Extend one arm forward with the palm facing up. Use the opposite hand to gently pull back the fingers to stretch the forearm. Hold for 15-20 seconds per hand.

C. Key Mobility Exercises for Disc Golf

Mobility exercises improve joint function and range of motion, enhancing the fluid rotation and dynamic movement required for disc golf throws.

- **Hip Circles** – Stand with feet shoulder-width apart, place hands on hips, and rotate in circular motions. Perform 10-15 rotations per direction to improve hip mobility.

- **World's Greatest Stretch** – Step into a lunge, lower the back knee, and twist toward the front leg while reaching up with the opposite arm. Perform 5-6 repetitions per side.

- **Spinal Roll** – Slowly roll down vertebra by vertebra, reaching for your toes, then roll back up. This improves spinal flexibility and mobility for smoother follow-throughs.

- **Ankle Mobility Drills** – Perform ankle circles or lunges with ankle flexion to enhance balance and stability in throwing stances.

- **Dynamic Shoulder Stretch** – Stand tall and cross your arms in front of your chest, then extend them outward. Repeat for 10-15 repetitions to improve shoulder mobility.

D. Integrating Flexibility & Mobility into Your Routine

To maximize the benefits of flexibility and mobility exercises, it's important to incorporate them into a structured routine that complements your disc golf training.

- **Warm-up before rounds** – Perform dynamic stretches, such as arm swings, leg kicks, and hip rotations, before starting your round to prepare your muscles for movement.

- **Cool-down after play** – After a round, focus on static stretching to help muscles recover and prevent tightness. This can include hamstring stretches, spinal twists, and shoulder stretches.

- **Daily mobility work** – Including 5-10 minutes of mobility drills each day helps maintain long-term flexibility and prevents stiffness, especially if you play frequently.

- **Target weak areas** – If you notice stiffness in specific areas, dedicate extra time to stretching and mobility drills that address those limitations.

E. Flexibility & Mobility for Injury Prevention

In addition to improving performance, flexibility and mobility exercises are crucial for injury prevention. Tight muscles and restricted joints are more prone to strains, sprains, and overuse injuries. By improving the flexibility and mobility of key muscle groups and joints, players can reduce their risk of injury and ensure long-term disc golf enjoyment.

- **Warm-up & cool-down** – Always incorporate dynamic stretches and mobility exercises into your warm-up before practice or a round, and perform static stretches after your round to cool down and prevent muscle tightness.

- **Listen to your body** – Pay attention to any areas of discomfort or tightness and address them with targeted stretches or mobility exercises. Over time, this will help prevent injuries and ensure that your body stays in optimal condition for throwing.

- **Avoid overuse** – While flexibility and mobility exercises are essential, it's also important not to overdo them. Balance stretching and mobility with adequate rest to allow the body to recover and prevent muscle strain or joint issues.

F. Key Takeaways

Flexibility and mobility are essential components of a well-rounded disc golf game, improving performance and reducing the risk of injury.

- **Flexibility exercises** – Stretch the shoulders, hamstrings, hips, and back for better range of motion and throwing mechanics.

- **Mobility exercises** – Improve joint function in the hips, spine, and ankles for smoother and more powerful movement.

- **Routine integration** – Warming up before play, cooling down after rounds, and incorporating daily mobility work ensures lasting benefits.

- **Injury prevention** – Consistently incorporating flexibility and mobility work reduces the risk of strains, overuse injuries, and stiffness.

By integrating these exercises into your routine, you'll improve your throwing mechanics, stay injury-free, and enhance your overall performance on the course. The next chapter will focus on strength training for distance and control, helping you build power for longer, more accurate throws.

7.3 Strength Training for Increased Distance & Control

Strength training plays a vital role in disc golf performance, particularly when it comes to increasing distance and control during throws. Building strength in key muscle groups—such as the legs, core, shoulders, and arms—improves your ability to generate power and enhances consistency in your throws. Stronger muscles allow you to maintain better form and control throughout the throwing motion, leading to more accurate and powerful shots. Additionally, strengthening the muscles used in disc golf helps reduce fatigue over multiple rounds, allowing players to sustain their performance longer. This section covers strength training exercises specifically designed for disc golf, helping you maximize your distance and control while reducing the risk of injury.

A strong core and upper body translate to greater throwing distance and control.

A. Why Strength Matters in Disc Golf

Strength is essential for generating power and stability during every throw. It enables you to throw longer distances with greater accuracy while protecting your body from strain and injury. A well-developed strength foundation allows players to execute throws more efficiently, leading to better consistency over time. Training key muscle groups not only enhances distance but also helps players maintain control under different playing conditions.

- **Generating power** – A powerful throw starts with a strong lower body and core. The legs and hips drive the motion, and the core transfers energy to the arms. Strengthening these areas allows you to generate more force and distance.

- **Control and consistency** – Stronger muscles stabilize your body during the throwing motion, giving you better control over the disc. With more control, your throws become more consistent, and you can fine-tune accuracy.

- **Injury prevention** – Strengthening the muscles used in throwing helps protect the joints and ligaments from repetitive stress. This reduces the risk of overuse injuries and improves longevity in the sport.

- **Endurance and efficiency** – Stronger muscles reduce fatigue during long rounds, allowing you to maintain power and control throughout the game.

B. Key Strength Training Exercises for Disc Golf

The following strength training exercises target major muscle groups involved in disc golf, improving both power and control. These exercises enhance your ability to generate force while maintaining accuracy and stability. Developing a strong, well-balanced body allows for better posture, smoother mechanics, and more efficient energy transfer in every throw.

- **Squats** – Build strength in the quads, glutes, and hamstrings, which generate power during the drive. Squats also improve balance and stability, ensuring proper body positioning.
  - o *How to perform*: Stand with feet shoulder-width apart, lower as if sitting in a chair, keeping back straight and knees aligned. Push through heels to return to the start. Perform 3 sets of 8-12 reps.
- **Deadlifts** – Strengthen the hamstrings, glutes, and lower back, which are key for driving power and stability in your throw.
  - o *How to perform*: Stand with feet shoulder-width apart, holding a barbell in front. Hinge at hips, lower the barbell, then lift by pushing through heels. Perform 3 sets of 6-8 reps.
- **Push-ups** – Strengthen the chest, shoulders, and triceps, which are critical for release and follow-through.
  - o *How to perform*: Start in a plank position with hands shoulder-width apart. Lower until your chest is just above the ground, then push back up. Perform 3 sets of 12-15 reps.
- **Pull-ups** – Target the upper back, shoulders, and biceps, improving pulling strength and control during follow-through.

- How to perform: Grab a pull-up bar with palms facing away, shoulder-width apart. Pull your chin above the bar, then lower slowly. Perform 3 sets of 5-8 reps.

C. Core Strength for Better Throws

Core strength is the foundation for every throw in disc golf. A strong core improves your ability to rotate through the throwing motion, generate power, and maintain balance. Since nearly all disc golf shots involve a rotational component, strengthening the core is crucial for maximizing throwing efficiency.

- **Russian Twists** – Target the obliques, essential for rotational power. Sit with knees bent, hold a weight, and twist from side to side. Perform 3 sets of 20 reps.

- **Planks** – Strengthen the entire core, including the abs, lower back, and obliques. Hold a plank position for 30-60 seconds, maintaining a straight line from head to heels. Perform 3-4 sets.

- **Medicine Ball Rotations** – Mimic the throwing motion and build core stability. Hold a medicine ball and rotate from side to side in a controlled motion. Perform 3 sets of 15-20 reps.

D. Strength Training for Injury Prevention

Strength training not only enhances performance but also helps prevent injuries. By reinforcing key muscle groups, you reduce strain on joints and improve overall resilience. Since disc golf involves repetitive motions, proper muscle conditioning minimizes the likelihood of overuse injuries that could sideline a player. Strengthening stabilizing muscles also supports better posture and reduces excessive stress on the lower back and shoulders.

- **Strengthening stabilizing muscles** – Exercises like deadlifts, squats, and planks help stabilize the spine, reducing the risk of back and hip injuries.

- **Balancing muscle development** – Strengthening opposing muscle groups (e.g., chest and back, quads and hamstrings) ensures muscle balance, reducing strain and improving movement efficiency.

- **Proper recovery and rest** – Allow muscles to recover between strength training sessions. Overtraining can lead to fatigue and increase the likelihood of injuries.

E. Structuring Your Strength Training Routine

To maximize the benefits of strength training, it's important to structure your workouts effectively. A well-balanced program will help you build power while maintaining mobility and endurance.

- **Train 2-3 times per week** – Focus on strength training sessions that target the major muscle groups used in disc golf. Allow time for recovery between workouts.

- **Incorporate full-body workouts** – Rather than isolating muscles, use compound exercises that engage multiple muscle groups, improving overall power and coordination.

- **Combine strength with mobility work** – Pair strength exercises with dynamic stretching and flexibility drills to ensure a full range of motion in your throws.

F. Key Takeaways

Strength training is vital for improving distance, accuracy, and control in disc golf. A well-structured strength program ensures players can generate power while maintaining precise mechanics throughout their throw.

- **Lower-body strength** – Squats and deadlifts build power in the legs and hips, essential for generating distance and stability.

- **Upper-body strength** – Push-ups, pull-ups, and overhead presses strengthen the shoulders and arms, improving control and follow-through.

- **Core strength** – Russian twists, planks, and medicine ball rotations enhance rotational power, balance, and stability.

- **Injury prevention** – Strength training protects joints and muscles, reducing strain and ensuring long-term performance.

By integrating these exercises into your fitness routine, you'll build the power and control necessary to increase distance and consistency in your disc golf game. The next chapter will focus on structuring training sessions effectively to maximize results.

7.4 Practicing With Purpose: How to Structure Your Training Sessions

To become a more skilled and effective disc golfer, practicing with purpose is essential. Simply throwing discs for hours without a focused plan won't help you improve as much as structured training sessions. Purposeful practice allows players to target specific areas of their game, track progress, and develop skills needed to perform under pressure. A well-planned session ensures that every aspect of the game—technique, strategy, conditioning, and mental preparation—is addressed systematically. By incorporating structured practice, players can enhance their technique, physical conditioning, and mental approach to disc golf, leading to better performance on the course.

Focused, structured training sessions lead to real improvements on the course.

A. Setting Specific Goals for Your Training

A successful training session begins with clear and specific goals. Goals provide direction, motivation, and measurable progress. Without them, it's easy to drift through training without making real improvements. Setting short-term and long-term goals ensures that every session is intentional and contributes to overall development. The best goals follow the **SMART** framework—Specific, Measurable, Achievable, Relevant, and Time-bound—so that improvement can be tracked and adjusted as needed.

- **Short-term goals** – Focus on specific skills to improve quickly, such as increasing putting accuracy, refining forehand technique, or improving consistency on approach shots.

- **Long-term goals** – Work toward broader achievements, like lowering your average score, mastering new throwing techniques, or preparing for competitive play.

- **SMART goals** – Goals should be structured for measurable improvement, such as increasing putting accuracy from 20 feet by 10% within four weeks or reducing average strokes per round by three over six months.

B. Creating a Balanced Practice Routine

Improvement in disc golf requires a well-rounded approach. A balanced practice routine includes skill development, physical conditioning, and mental training. Many players focus only on throwing, but improving endurance, strength, and mental resilience is just as important. Dividing practice sessions into dedicated blocks helps ensure that all aspects of the game receive attention.

- **Throwing technique practice** – Work on various types of throws: backhands, forehands, putting, and specialty shots like rollers or overhands. Each type of throw requires different mechanics, and focusing on one per session allows for deeper improvement.

- o **Drill progression** – Start with form-based drills, then move to advanced accuracy and distance drills.
- o **Targeted practice** – Break up throwing practice into dedicated blocks, such as 30 minutes of forehand throws, 20 minutes of putting, and 15 minutes of accuracy drills.
- **Physical conditioning** – Strength, flexibility, and endurance training play a significant role in consistency and injury prevention. Aim for 2-3 sessions per week focusing on:
  - o Strength training for power (e.g., squats, lunges, and core exercises).
  - o Mobility exercises to increase range of motion.
  - o Endurance training for long rounds.
- **Mental focus and strategy** – Disc golf requires mental resilience. Simulating high-pressure situations, practicing visualization, and focusing on shot selection help improve decision-making on the course.

C. Structuring Your Training Sessions

To get the most from each practice session, structure it with clear segments. A well-structured session includes warm-ups, focused drills, physical conditioning, and a cool-down to maximize improvement and prevent injuries.

- **Warm-up (10-15 minutes)**
  - o **Dynamic stretching** – Activate muscles with movements like arm circles, leg swings, and torso twists.
  - o **Light throwing drills** – Begin with short, controlled throws to reinforce mechanics and loosen up muscles.
- **Skill development (30-45 minutes)**

- o **Focused drills** – Work on a specific skill such as putting consistency, distance driving, or controlled forehand throws.

  - o **Game-simulation practice** – Set up real-course conditions, like throwing around obstacles or practicing approach shots from various lies.

- **Conditioning (15-20 minutes)**

  - o **Strength exercises** – Incorporate movements that target disc golf-specific muscles (e.g., squats, deadlifts, shoulder presses).

  - o **Flexibility training** – Include yoga-style stretches to maintain range of motion and prevent tightness.

- **Cool-down (5-10 minutes)**

  - o **Static stretching** – Hold stretches for 20-30 seconds to improve flexibility and aid recovery.

  - o **Reflection** – Note what went well, what needs work, and set goals for the next session.

D. Tracking Progress and Adjusting Your Plan

To ensure continued growth, tracking progress is key. Without data, it's difficult to identify what's improving and where adjustments are needed. Keeping a training log helps players evaluate their performance and modify their practice sessions for better results.

- **Log your training sessions** – Write down drills, results, and observations. Tracking performance provides motivation and highlights improvement areas.

- **Assess performance regularly** – Every few weeks, review whether goals are being met. If progress stalls, adjust training intensity, frequency, or focus.

- **Modify the plan** – If putting improves but driving distance lags, shift focus to form and power drills for distance throws.

Example of a training log entry:

- **Date:** March 11

- **Focus:** Forehand distance and putting

- **Results:** 60% putting accuracy from 25 feet (goal: 70% by April), forehand throws reached an average of 250 feet (goal: 275 feet by next month)

- **Adjustments needed:** More reps on forehand technique drills, add more wrist control exercises

E. Incorporating Real-Game Scenarios

Practicing under real-game conditions helps bridge the gap between training and actual performance. Too often, players perform well in casual practice but struggle under tournament pressure. Simulating real-game situations builds confidence and improves adaptability.

- **Course-specific challenges** – Practice shots from uneven terrain, wooded areas, and windy conditions to simulate real play.

- **Pressure situations** – Set up drills where you must make a final putt or complete a hole with a limited number of strokes to create tournament-like stress.

- **Shot selection drills** – Give yourself multiple options for a shot and choose the best one, reinforcing strategic thinking on the course.

F. Common Practice Mistakes and How to Avoid Them

Many players practice inefficiently without realizing it. Avoid these mistakes to maximize improvement:

- **Mindless repetition** – Throwing discs repeatedly without focus doesn't improve skills. Always have a goal and track results.

- **Skipping weak areas** – It's natural to practice what you're good at, but improvement comes from working on weaknesses. Allocate time to all aspects of your game.

- **Ignoring mental training** – The mental side of disc golf is crucial. Visualization and pressure drills help prepare for real competition.

G. Key Takeaways

Purposeful practice is the key to improving your disc golf skills and performance.

- **Set clear goals** – Define short-term and long-term objectives to guide training.

- **Balance training** – Include throwing drills, conditioning, and mental exercises in your routine.

- **Structure sessions effectively** – Use a warm-up, skill drills, conditioning, and a cool-down to maximize productivity.

- **Track and adjust** – Monitor progress, identify weak areas, and refine your training plan.

- **Practice real-game scenarios** – Train under conditions that mimic tournament play for better preparation.

By structuring your practice sessions effectively and tracking progress, you'll accelerate your improvement and develop a stronger, more consistent disc golf game. The next chapter will focus on preparing for tournaments and competitive play, helping you transition from practice to high-level performance.

Chapter 7 Review: Training, Fitness & Disc Golf Performance

Chapter 7 emphasizes the importance of physical conditioning and structured training in improving your disc golf game. Strength, flexibility, endurance, and core stability all play a role in developing better control, power, and consistency. This chapter covers disc golf-specific workouts that enhance throwing mechanics, prevent injuries, and build stamina for long rounds. Additionally, it explores how to structure purposeful practice, ensuring that every training session is focused and effective. With a combination of physical fitness and targeted drills, players can maximize their potential and sustain peak performance on the course.

7.1 Disc Golf-Specific Workouts for Power & Endurance

- **Power workouts** – Medicine ball slams, kettlebell swings, and box jumps build explosive strength in the legs, core, and shoulders, increasing throwing power.

- **Endurance workouts** – Circuit training, running, and cycling enhance stamina, helping players maintain focus and energy throughout a full round.

- **Core workouts** – Russian twists, planks, and deadbugs strengthen rotational stability, improving control and accuracy in throws.

7.2 Flexibility & Mobility Exercises for Better Throws

- **Shoulder and hip mobility drills** – Shoulder rotations, hip circles, and dynamic stretches enhance flexibility and prevent stiffness in key throwing areas.

- **Yoga and stretching** – Improves range of motion, increases balance, and reduces injury risk, making movements smoother and more efficient.

- **Foam rolling and recovery techniques** – Helps release muscle tension, improve blood flow, and maintain flexibility in the lower back, legs, and shoulders.

7.3 Strength Training for Increased Distance & Control

- **Leg and core strength** – Squats, deadlifts, and lunges build lower-body power, improving throwing stability and follow-through control.

- **Upper body training** – Push-ups, pull-ups, and overhead presses strengthen the arms and shoulders, increasing throwing force and endurance.

- **Grip strength exercises** – Wrist curls, farmer's carries, and resistance bands improve grip stability, reducing release inconsistencies.

7.4 Practicing with Purpose: How to Structure Your Training Sessions

- **Goal setting** – Define clear, measurable goals for distance, accuracy, and endurance to track progress.

- **Balanced training** – Combine technical skill development, conditioning, and mental practice to improve all aspects of the game.

- **Structured practice sessions** – Warm up, focus on mechanics, incorporate conditioning, and finish with cooldown exercises for a complete training routine.

- **Tracking progress** – Logging results and analyzing performance helps players refine techniques and adapt their training for continued growth.

Chapter 7 provides a comprehensive guide to improving disc golf performance through fitness and structured training. By incorporating strength training, flexibility exercises, and purposeful practice, players can build a solid foundation for increased power, endurance, and consistency. The next chapter explores how to prepare for tournaments and competitive play, equipping players with the strategies and mindset to perform under pressure.

Chapter 8: Tournaments & Competitive Play

Competing in disc golf tournaments requires preparation, strategy, and mental toughness. Whether you're entering your first event or refining your competitive mindset, this chapter covers everything you need to succeed. You'll get an introduction to the Professional Disc Golf Association (PDGA) and the different tournament formats, along with guidance on how to get started. Preparation is key, so we'll explore physical and mental strategies to help you stay focused and confident. You'll also learn essential tournament rules, etiquette, and techniques for managing pressure in high-stakes situations. By mastering these elements, you'll be ready to compete with confidence and take your game to the next level.

Competing in tournaments sharpens your skills and pushes you to the next level.

8.1 The PDGA & Disc Golf Tournaments: How to Get Started

Getting involved in disc golf tournaments is an exciting step for players looking to challenge themselves and take their game to the next level. The Professional Disc Golf Association (PDGA) is the governing body for the sport, organizing tournaments and setting rules for play at all levels, from recreational events to professional competitions. Whether you're a newcomer or an experienced player, participating in tournaments offers valuable experience and a sense of community. This section will guide you through getting started, from registering for your first event to understanding tournament formats and the PDGA structure.

The PDGA is your gateway to organized disc golf—start competing today.

A. The PDGA: What Is It and Why It Matters

The PDGA is the official organization responsible for maintaining the rules of disc golf and promoting the sport worldwide. It organizes events, maintains player rankings, and provides official guidelines for competition.

- **Establishing the rules** – The PDGA ensures a standardized experience for players at all levels by setting official rules that cover everything from scoring to course design and tournament formats.

- **Membership benefits** – While non-members can participate in tournaments, PDGA members receive benefits such as access to official events, player rankings, and discounts on disc golf gear. Members also receive a PDGA number that tracks their tournament history and performance.

- **Player rankings** – The PDGA tracks sanctioned event performance, allowing players to build competitive rankings. Higher rankings can influence tournament eligibility and seeding.

- **Tournament sanctioning** – The PDGA sanctions events to ensure they meet specific standards, including course layouts, official rules, and player conduct.

B. How to Register for Your First Tournament

Entering your first disc golf tournament can feel intimidating, but it's a straightforward process. Here's how to get started:

- **Find a local tournament** – Start with beginner-friendly PDGA-sanctioned tournaments, often hosted by disc golf clubs and courses. These events allow you to gain experience in a welcoming environment.

- **Register online** – Most tournaments require online registration through the PDGA website or a tournament-specific page. Fill out the form, pay the entry fee, and check the registration deadlines, as spots may be limited. Some larger tournaments fill up quickly, so early registration is recommended.

- **Choose your division** – Divisions are based on skill level and gender. Beginners typically start in the recreational or novice division, progressing to intermediate and advanced as they improve. Choosing the correct division ensures a fair and competitive playing experience.

- **Understand the format** – Tournaments vary in format, from one-day to multi-day events. Most PDGA events follow a stroke-play format, where players complete the course in the fewest strokes. Some feature match play or doubles formats, so review event details when signing up.

C. Types of Disc Golf Tournaments

Disc golf tournaments cater to players of all skill levels, from casual events to professional competitions. Understanding the different types of tournaments will help you find events that match your experience level and goals.

- **Local and club events** – Beginner-friendly tournaments that provide a relaxed environment for learning and meeting fellow players. These events often have lower entry fees and a fun atmosphere, making them ideal for newcomers.

- **PDGA Sanctioned Events** – Competitive tournaments following official PDGA rules, where players earn points toward their rankings. These range from small local competitions to regional and national events.

- **National Tour and Major Events** – High-level competitions featuring elite players and larger prize pools. Events like the PDGA National Tour and World Championships are goals for competitive disc golfers.

D. What to Expect at Your First Tournament

Entering a tournament for the first time can be an exciting and nerve-wracking experience. Here's what to expect:

- **Check-in and registration** – Arrive early to check in, receive your player pack (which may include a tournament disc, scorecard, and event schedule), and confirm your tee time.

- **Tee times and groupings** – Players are grouped by division and tee off in groups of 3-4. You'll likely be paired with others at your skill level.

- **Course layout and rules** – Study the course layout and review any tournament-specific rules, such as out-of-bounds areas and mandatory lines. Understanding these rules will prevent unnecessary penalties.

E. Tips for First-Time Tournament Players

Your first tournament should be an enjoyable learning experience. Keep these tips in mind to make the most of it:

- **Stay relaxed** – Don't pressure yourself to perform perfectly. Treat your first tournament as an opportunity to gain experience.

- **Be respectful** – Follow proper course etiquette, respect fellow players, and adhere to pace-of-play guidelines. Maintain good sportsmanship regardless of how well you play.

- **Bring the essentials** – Pack plenty of water, snacks, extra discs, comfortable shoes, sunscreen, and weather-appropriate gear.

- **Observe experienced players** – Learn from how seasoned players handle pressure, approach their shots, and navigate the course.

- **Stick to your game plan** – Avoid changing your throwing technique or strategy just because you're in a competitive setting.

F. Preparing Mentally for Competition

The mental aspect of disc golf is just as important as physical preparation. Handling nerves and staying focused will help you perform well under pressure.

- **Visualization techniques** – Before each round, visualize your ideal shots and outcomes. This helps build confidence and reduces anxiety.

- **Focus on one shot at a time** – Avoid worrying about your overall score. Concentrate on executing each shot to the best of your ability.

- **Stay positive** – Bad shots happen to everyone. Instead of dwelling on mistakes, focus on the next opportunity to make a great shot.

G. Key Takeaways

Getting involved in disc golf tournaments is an exciting way to challenge yourself and progress as a player.

- **The PDGA** – The Professional Disc Golf Association governs the sport, organizes events, and tracks rankings.

- **Tournament registration** – To compete, find a local event, register online, choose your division, and understand the format.

- **Types of tournaments** – Tournaments range from casual local events to elite-level PDGA competitions.

- **First tournament expectations** – Arrive early, familiarize yourself with the course, and focus on enjoying the experience.

- **Tips for success** – Stay relaxed, bring necessary gear, and use your first tournament as an opportunity to grow.

- **Mental preparation** – Confidence, focus, and a positive mindset will help you stay composed during competition.

By understanding the tournament structure and preparing properly, you can transition smoothly into competitive play and gain valuable experience. Whether you're playing for fun or aiming to improve your ranking, participating in tournaments is a great way to test your skills, meet fellow players, and push yourself to new levels. The next section will focus on preparing for competition, covering strategies to enhance both physical and mental readiness for tournament success.

8.2 Preparing for Competition: Physical & Mental Readiness

Competing in disc golf tournaments requires more than just technical skill; it demands physical conditioning and mental preparation to perform at your best under pressure. This section will explore how to prepare physically by enhancing your endurance, strength, and flexibility, as well as how to sharpen your mental focus to stay composed during challenging tournament situations. Developing both aspects of your game will give you the confidence and stamina needed to succeed in competitive play.

Prepare both physically and mentally to perform your best when it matters most.

A. Physical Readiness for Tournament Play

Physical readiness is crucial for maintaining energy levels, executing accurate throws, and preventing injury throughout the duration of a tournament. Disc golf tournaments can last several hours, and staying physically prepared will help you perform consistently, especially during long rounds.

- **Endurance training** – Disc golf requires sustained energy and stamina. To improve your endurance, incorporate cardiovascular exercises such as running, cycling, or hiking into your training routine. Aim for 2-3 cardio sessions per week, each lasting 30-45 minutes. The better your cardiovascular fitness, the less fatigued you'll feel after multiple rounds and long days on the course.

- **Strength and flexibility** – Building strength in key muscle groups, such as the legs, core, and shoulders, is essential for maintaining control and power in your throws. Strength training exercises like squats, deadlifts, and core exercises will help you maintain your form throughout the round. Flexibility exercises like yoga or dynamic stretching will improve your range of motion, allowing you to throw more efficiently and avoid muscle strain during the competition.

- **Core stability** – A strong core is fundamental for generating power and stability during your throws. Incorporate exercises like planks, Russian twists, and dead bugs into your training to enhance your rotational strength, which directly impacts your throwing mechanics.

- **Nutrition and hydration** – Proper nutrition and hydration are essential for keeping your energy levels up throughout the tournament. Make sure to eat balanced meals that provide long-lasting energy, such as complex carbs, protein, and healthy fats. Drink plenty of water before, during, and after rounds to stay hydrated and avoid fatigue.

B. Mental Readiness for Tournament Play

Mental readiness is equally important as physical preparation in disc golf. Tournament play often involves handling pressure, staying focused for long hours, and maintaining composure through the ups and downs of competition. Preparing mentally for a tournament will help you stay confident and focused when faced with tough situations.

- **Visualization** – Visualization is a powerful tool used by professional athletes to enhance performance. Before the tournament, take time to visualize yourself on the course, imagining each throw and how you'll handle various challenges. Visualizing success can help build confidence and reduce anxiety by mentally preparing you for each aspect of the round. Spend a few minutes each day imagining yourself executing perfect shots and feeling composed under pressure.

- **Breathing exercises** – Deep breathing exercises can help calm nerves and focus your mind, especially when dealing with tournament anxiety or a difficult stretch during the round.

Practice slow, controlled breathing to relax your body and clear your mind. You can use these techniques in between holes or during a stressful situation on the course.

- **Positive self-talk** – Disc golfers often experience highs and lows throughout a tournament. Practicing positive self-talk is essential for maintaining your focus and staying mentally strong. When facing adversity, remind yourself that you're capable of handling challenges. Phrases like "I can do this" or "I'm staying focused" can reinforce a positive mindset and keep negative thoughts at bay.

- **Pre-round routines** – A consistent pre-round routine can help you enter the competition with the right mindset. Whether it's reviewing your game plan, performing a warm-up routine, or mentally rehearsing your shots, having a set routine will help you feel grounded and focused before your round begins.

- **Handling nerves** – Nerves are a natural part of competition, but learning to control them is crucial. Developing relaxation techniques such as deep breathing, progressive muscle relaxation, and staying present in the moment can help you manage anxiety and perform under pressure. Focus on your process, not the outcome, and stay committed to executing each shot to the best of your ability.

C. Combining Physical and Mental Readiness

Physical and mental readiness go hand in hand in competitive play. One aspect cannot be fully effective without the other, so it's essential to prepare both your body and mind for tournament play. Here's how to combine the two:

- **Holistic approach** – Treat your preparation as a balanced approach, where physical and mental conditioning support each other. A physically prepared body allows you to execute techniques with precision, while a strong mindset helps you stay focused and confident throughout the tournament.

- **Training under pressure** – In your practice sessions, simulate tournament conditions by adding pressure. Practice shots under time constraints or with distractions to replicate the mental pressure of a real tournament. This will help you build mental toughness and resilience.

- **Adaptability** – Be flexible in your approach to both the physical and mental aspects of your game. Each tournament and course will present different challenges, and being able to adjust to those challenges while staying physically and mentally sharp is key to long-term success in competitive play.

D. Key Takeaways

Tournament play requires both physical and mental preparation for optimal performance.

- **Physical preparation** – Build endurance, strength, and flexibility through consistent training. Focus on core stability, nutrition, and hydration to maintain energy and prevent injury.

- **Mental preparation** – Use visualization, positive self-talk, and breathing exercises to stay focused and manage nerves during the tournament.

- **Combining both aspects** – A well-rounded preparation plan incorporates both physical conditioning and mental readiness, ensuring you are fully prepared for the challenges of competition.

- **Pre-round routines** – Establish routines to help you mentally and physically prepare for each round, enhancing focus and confidence.

By preparing your body and mind for competition, you can perform confidently under tournament conditions and handle the pressure that comes with competitive play. In the next chapter, we will explore the rules, etiquette, and strategies for playing in tournaments, helping you navigate the competitive disc golf environment with ease.

8.3 Tournament Rules & Etiquette: What to Expect

Understanding tournament rules and proper etiquette is essential for a successful disc golf experience. Whether you're playing in a local tournament or a national event, knowing the official rules and adhering to course etiquette ensures a fair, respectful, and enjoyable competition. A well-run tournament depends on all players following the rules and maintaining good sportsmanship. This section covers key tournament rules and etiquette expectations, helping you navigate competitive play with confidence and respect.

Knowing the rules and etiquette ensures a smooth and fair competition experience.

A. Official Tournament Rules

Disc golf tournaments follow the official rules established by the Professional Disc Golf Association (PDGA). These guidelines ensure fair competition, consistency across events, and smooth gameplay for all participants. Whether you are a first-time competitor or a seasoned player, following these rules will improve your experience and help prevent penalties.

- **Stroke Play** – The most common format where total throws determine the winner. The player with the fewest strokes at the end of the round wins. Some tournaments consist of multiple rounds played over one or more days.

- **Out-of-Bounds (OB) Rules** – If a disc lands in an OB area, such as water or roads, a penalty stroke is added, and the player must throw from the last inbounds position. Some courses have designated drop zones.

- **Mandatories (Mandos)** – Certain holes require players to throw around specific obstacles. Missing a mando results in a penalty stroke and a rethrow from a designated drop zone.

- **Teeing Off** – Players must tee off from designated tee pads in the correct order. Some tournaments use assigned tee times, while others use a shotgun start, where players begin on different holes at the same time.

- **Scorekeeping & Digital Scoring** – Players must track their scores and those of their group members. Many tournaments use digital scoring, but players should still confirm scores before submission to avoid mistakes.

B. Tournament Etiquette

Proper etiquette ensures fair play and a positive experience for all competitors. Respecting other players, maintaining pace, and upholding the spirit of the game make for a better tournament environment.

- **Respect Pace of Play** – Be ready to throw when it's your turn and avoid unnecessary delays. If a disc is lost, the group should assist in searching while keeping track of the time limit.

- **Stay Quiet & Still** – Avoid talking or moving while others are throwing. Unnecessary noise can be distracting, especially on putts.

- **Give Personal Space** – Stand clear of a player's throwing line and avoid obstructing their view of the basket. Position yourself where you won't interfere with their shot.

- **Follow Course Rules** – Keep the course clean, avoid damaging trees or baskets, and respect posted guidelines. Many courses are maintained by volunteers, so being mindful of your surroundings helps preserve the game.

- **Show Good Sportsmanship** – Congratulate good shots, accept rulings without argument, and encourage fair play. Even in a competitive setting, maintaining a positive attitude fosters camaraderie.

C. What to Expect in a Tournament Setting

Tournaments have a structured format, and understanding the process will help you feel more confident. Being prepared ensures a smoother and more enjoyable experience.

- **Check-In & Player Packs** – Players check in before the round and may receive a tournament disc, scorecard, or other event materials. Some larger tournaments also provide welcome packages with sponsor gifts.

- **Tee Assignments & Course Prep** – Some tournaments assign tee times, while others use shotgun starts. Players should arrive early to warm up and check the course layout. Reviewing the course map and hole distances can help with shot selection.

- **Group Play** – Players are grouped by skill level or division, typically in groups of three or four. Playing with similarly skilled competitors ensures a fair and competitive experience.

- **Round Duration** – Tournament rounds often take longer than casual rounds due to scorekeeping, larger player fields, and increased focus on execution. Expect a round to last three to four hours, depending on the course and conditions.

D. Handling Rules Disputes & Calling Violations

Rules disputes can arise, and knowing how to handle them professionally ensures fairness. Disc golf relies on self-officiating, meaning players must uphold and enforce rules when necessary.

- **Addressing Violations** – If a rule is broken, calmly inform the player and discuss the ruling with the group.

- **Consulting the Tournament Director** – If there's disagreement, the tournament director will clarify the rule and make a final decision. Their ruling is final and should be accepted without argument.

- **Honesty & Self-Officiating** – Players should call penalties on themselves if they make an error. Integrity is a core value in disc golf competition, and self-officiating is an important part of tournament play.

E. How to Stay Mentally Composed During Tournament Play

Tournaments bring added pressure compared to casual rounds, but staying mentally composed will help you perform at your best. Disc golf requires mental discipline, and handling pressure effectively is a skill that top players develop over time.

- **Use a Pre-Shot Routine** – Developing a consistent pre-shot routine, such as taking a deep breath or visualizing the throw, helps maintain focus and confidence.

- **Focus on One Shot at a Time** – Avoid stressing over your total score and concentrate on executing each throw to the best of your ability.

- **Control Emotions** – Whether you make a great shot or a mistake, staying calm is essential. Emotional control can prevent rushed decisions and keep you in a positive mindset.

- **Stay Hydrated & Fueled** – Tournament rounds can be long, so bring water and snacks to maintain energy levels and concentration.

- **Move On from Mistakes** – Every player makes errors, but the ability to reset mentally and focus on the next throw is crucial for success.

F. Key Takeaways

Tournament rules and etiquette ensure a fair and enjoyable experience for all players.

- **Know the rules** – Understanding PDGA regulations helps prevent penalties and disputes.

- **Respect the game** – Good etiquette includes maintaining pace, staying quiet, and showing sportsmanship.

- **Prepare for the setting** – Arrive early, review the course, and know your tee time and group assignment.

- **Resolve disputes fairly** – Handle rule concerns calmly and consult the tournament director when necessary.

- **Stay mentally strong** – Focus on one shot at a time, maintain composure, and be prepared physically and mentally.

- **Adapt to tournament conditions** – Each tournament presents unique challenges—adjust your strategy and mindset accordingly.

By following these guidelines, you'll be ready to compete with confidence while ensuring an enjoyable experience for yourself and fellow players. The next chapter will focus on strategies for handling pressure and performing well in high-stakes situations.

8.4 Playing Under Pressure: Handling Nerves & High-Stakes Situations

Tournament play often brings with it high-pressure situations where the stakes are elevated, and every shot feels crucial. Handling nerves and maintaining focus under pressure are key skills that can make the difference between winning and losing. This section explores strategies for managing stress, staying calm, and performing at your best when faced with high-stakes moments in disc golf. Whether you're in a tight competition or facing a difficult hole, the ability to stay composed and execute under pressure is essential for success.

Stay calm under pressure and trust your routine—every shot counts in competition.

A. Recognizing and Managing Tournament Nerves

Feeling nervous before or during a tournament is completely natural. Nerves can arise from the pressure to perform well, the competitive atmosphere, or even the fear of making mistakes. However, learning how to manage these nerves effectively can help you stay focused and perform your best.

- **Acknowledge your nerves** – The first step to managing nerves is to recognize and accept that they're a normal part of the competition. Everyone experiences anxiety or pressure during tournaments, but by acknowledging it, you take away its power. Understanding that it's a natural reaction will help you stay calm and focused.

- **Deep breathing** – Deep breathing exercises are one of the most effective ways to calm the mind and body. Practice slow, deep breaths in through your nose, holding for a few seconds, and then exhaling slowly through your mouth. This helps lower your heart rate, reduce muscle tension, and focus your attention.

- **Focus on the process, not the outcome** – Often, nerves arise when you focus too much on the outcome—such as worrying about winning, making a mistake, or the score. Instead, shift your focus to the process. Concentrate on executing each shot with the best form and technique you can muster, rather than obsessing over the result. This shift in perspective helps reduce pressure and keeps your attention on what you can control.

- **Use positive self-talk** – Remind yourself that you're capable of handling the pressure. Positive affirmations like "I've done this before" or "I'm in control" can boost your confidence and focus. Repeating these statements in your head helps keep negative thoughts at bay and empowers you to stay composed under pressure.

B. Staying Calm During High-Stakes Moments

There will inevitably be high-stakes moments during tournaments—perhaps a crucial putt to win the round or a difficult shot in a tight situation. These moments can trigger nerves, but learning how to stay calm and collected will help you make your best decisions and execute effectively.

- **Stay in the present** – One of the most effective ways to stay calm is to remain fully present in the moment. Avoid thinking about past mistakes or worrying about what will happen next. Focus on the current shot, the current hole, and what you need to do to succeed. This present-moment awareness helps reduce distractions and keeps you calm under pressure.

- **Break it down** – Large, intimidating situations can feel overwhelming, especially in tournament play. Break them down into smaller, manageable parts. For example, if you have a difficult putt, focus on the fundamentals—your stance, grip, and alignment—rather than thinking about the pressure of the moment. By narrowing your focus to these elements, you can reduce anxiety and execute with precision.

- **Visualize success** – Before taking a high-stakes shot, take a moment to visualize the shot going well. Imagine yourself making a perfect throw or sinking the putt. Visualizing success builds confidence and can help reduce anxiety by mentally preparing you for the situation. The more vividly you can picture it, the more likely you are to execute it successfully.

C. Techniques for Playing in High-Pressure Situations

As you encounter higher-pressure situations, whether in a tight match or during a difficult hole, it's important to have strategies in place to handle them effectively. The following techniques will help you manage the pressure and stay focused on your game.

- **Develop a pre-shot routine** – A consistent pre-shot routine can help you feel more in control and less rushed when you're under pressure. Take the time to gather yourself, focus on your breathing, and visualize your shot before stepping up to the tee. A routine creates consistency and reduces distractions, helping you maintain focus and composure.

- **Control your body language** – Your body language can influence your mental state. Maintaining relaxed and confident body language—such as standing tall, breathing deeply, and keeping a calm demeanor—can help reduce stress and send positive signals to your mind. Conversely, slumping or appearing tense can increase feelings of anxiety.

- **Focus on one shot at a time** – During high-pressure moments, it's easy to start thinking about the entire round or the outcome of the tournament. Instead, focus on the task at hand: making your next shot. By taking it one shot at a time, you can reduce overwhelming feelings and stay grounded.

- **Stay positive after mistakes** – Mistakes are inevitable, but how you react to them can make all the difference. If you make an error, acknowledge it, learn from it, and then let it go. Refocus and move forward with a positive attitude. This resilience helps maintain your confidence throughout the tournament.

D. Key Takeaways

Handling nerves and performing under pressure are essential skills for tournament success in disc golf.

- **Acknowledge your nerves** – Recognize that feeling nervous is normal and part of the competition. Accept it and use it as a motivator.

- **Deep breathing** – Practice slow, deep breathing exercises to calm your body and focus your mind.

- **Focus on the process** – Shift your attention from the outcome to the execution of each shot, helping you stay in control.

- **Stay present and break it down** – Focus on the present moment and break high-pressure situations into smaller, manageable tasks.

- **Positive self-talk** – Use affirmations and visualize success to build confidence and reduce anxiety.

- **Pre-shot routine** – Develop a consistent routine to create focus and consistency in your play, especially under pressure.

By applying these strategies, you can stay calm and perform at your best during high-pressure situations in tournaments. In the next chapter, we'll explore the mental game in more detail, focusing on techniques for maintaining focus, developing resilience, and staying confident during the entirety of your round.

Chapter 8 Review: Tournaments & Competitive Play

Chapter 8 focuses on preparing players for disc golf tournaments, offering valuable insights into navigating the world of competitive play. It covers the essential steps for getting started, from registering for your first PDGA event to understanding tournament rules and etiquette. Additionally, the chapter emphasizes physical and mental readiness, helping players build the endurance, strength, and mindset needed to handle high-pressure situations. Whether you're new to tournaments or looking to refine your approach, this chapter provides the knowledge to compete with confidence.

8.1 The PDGA & Disc Golf Tournaments: How to Get Started

- **PDGA membership** – Joining the PDGA allows players to participate in sanctioned events, track performance, and earn player ratings.

- **Registration process** – Players can find local, regional, and national tournaments through PDGA resources and register in their appropriate division.

- **Tournament levels** – PDGA events range from casual local competitions to elite-level championships, catering to all skill levels.

8.2 Preparing for Competition: Physical & Mental Readiness

- **Endurance training** – Long tournament rounds require cardiovascular fitness, making running, hiking, and interval training beneficial.

- **Strength and flexibility** – Exercises like squats, core workouts, and shoulder mobility drills improve power and throwing consistency.

- **Mental preparation** – Techniques like visualization, deep breathing, and positive self-talk help players stay calm and focused under pressure.

- **Practice rounds** – Playing the tournament course beforehand helps familiarize players with fairways, hazards, and ideal shot placements.

8.3 Tournament Rules & Etiquette: What to Expect

- **Stroke play format** – The most common tournament style where players compete for the lowest total strokes.

- **Course-specific rules** – Understanding out-of-bounds areas, mandatories, and penalty strokes ensures compliance with tournament regulations.

- **Etiquette and sportsmanship** – Maintaining silence during throws, respecting pace of play, and showing good sportsmanship create a positive tournament atmosphere.

- **Group responsibilities** – Players must keep score, call penalties, and uphold the integrity of the game.

8.4 Playing Under Pressure: Handling Nerves & High-Stakes Situations

- **Managing nerves** – Breathing techniques, pre-shot routines, and focusing on execution rather than outcome help reduce anxiety.

- **Building confidence** – Trusting in practice, maintaining consistent mechanics, and using positive reinforcement lead to better performance.

- **Recovering from mistakes** – A strong mental game allows players to move past bad shots, refocus, and finish rounds with confidence.

Chapter 8 provides a complete guide to tournament preparation, covering the rules, strategies, and mindset needed to compete successfully. The next chapter explores the mental game in greater depth, offering advanced techniques for staying focused and performing at your best throughout a competition.

Chapter 9: The Mental Game – How to Stay Focused & Confident

The mental side of disc golf is just as important as physical skill, especially in competitive play. Staying focused, calm, and confident can be the difference between winning and losing. This chapter covers how to manage pressure, build mental resilience, and develop a strong routine for consistent performance. You'll learn techniques like visualization and mental rehearsal to prepare for peak performance. Additionally, we'll explore strategies for rebounding after a bad throw, helping you stay composed and focused throughout a round. By mastering the mental game, you'll improve decision-making, handle pressure with ease, and play your best when it matters most.

A strong mental game is the key to consistency, confidence, and peak performance.

9.1 Managing Pressure & Tournament Nerves

Feeling nervous or anxious before and during a tournament is completely normal, especially when there's a lot on the line. However, how you handle those nerves and pressure can significantly impact your performance. Managing pressure in disc golf is all about developing strategies to stay calm, focused, and in control of your game, even when the stakes are high. This section explores techniques for recognizing, understanding, and managing tournament nerves, helping you stay composed and perform at your best, regardless of the situation.

Learn to manage nerves so they don't control your performance on the course.

A. Understanding the Source of Tournament Nerves

Nerves and pressure often arise from various sources during tournament play. Understanding where these feelings come from is the first step toward managing them effectively. Many players feel pressure due to high expectations, fear of failure, or the desire to perform well. Identifying the root causes helps in developing targeted strategies to manage anxiety before and during the competition.

- **Fear of failure** – The desire to perform well can lead to a fear of making mistakes. This fear often manifests as nervousness, especially when players feel they have something to prove. The pressure to meet personal or external expectations can create performance anxiety, which affects concentration and focus.

- **Competition anxiety** – The competitive environment can make players feel self-conscious or intimidated, particularly when facing more experienced players. Being under the spotlight, or simply participating in a highly competitive event, can heighten stress and nerves, influencing the player's ability to focus and perform.

- **Desire to win** – The greater the stakes, the more pressure players feel to perform. Whether it's a local tournament or a major event, the desire to win or achieve a personal best can exacerbate feelings of anxiety, leading players to overthink and lose focus.

B. Techniques for Managing Pressure

There are several proven techniques that can help players stay calm and collected under pressure, allowing them to perform at their best despite the stress of the competition. These strategies help reduce anxiety and maintain focus on the task at hand, ensuring that nerves do not interfere with execution.

- **Breathing exercises** – Deep, controlled breathing is one of the most effective ways to calm nerves and reduce anxiety. By focusing on slow, steady breaths, players can activate their body's relaxation response. Practicing this method before and during a round can help regulate heart rate and clear the mind, keeping players calm and focused.

- **Visualization** – Visualization is a powerful mental tool that helps athletes mentally rehearse success. Taking a few moments to close your eyes and visualize yourself executing perfect throws or making successful putts boosts confidence and reduces anxiety. This mental practice prepares the brain to handle pressure by associating calm and control with competition situations.

- **Mindfulness** – Mindfulness techniques help players remain in the present moment, preventing them from dwelling on past mistakes or worrying about the future. By focusing solely on the current shot, players can clear their minds of distractions and stay fully engaged in the task. Mindfulness promotes mental clarity and emotional control, essential components of tournament performance.

C. Shifting Focus to the Process, Not the Outcome

Shifting focus from the outcome to the process is a highly effective strategy for managing pressure in tournament play. Worrying about the result often leads to stress and performance anxiety. Instead, focusing on actions within your control—such as your technique, form, and execution—helps you remain calm and concentrate on what matters most.

- **Focus on the shot, not the score** – Concentrate on executing each shot to the best of your ability, rather than stressing over the potential impact on your score or position in the tournament. Focusing on the shot itself, including the grip, stance, and follow-through, helps players stay grounded and focused on their form, which reduces the mental clutter caused by outcome-based thinking.

- **Take one shot at a time** – Instead of focusing on the entire round or worrying about past mistakes, players should focus on the present shot. By concentrating on the next shot, players eliminate the pressure of future outcomes and free themselves from negative thoughts. This approach keeps the player focused on the moment, which aids in performance.

- **Break the round into segments** – Breaking the round into smaller, manageable segments can alleviate the stress of thinking about the full course or tournament. By focusing on individual holes and treating each as a separate challenge, players can reduce the feeling of being overwhelmed, making the competition feel more attainable.

D. Handling Mistakes and Staying Calm

Mistakes are an inevitable part of the game, and how you handle them can significantly influence the remainder of your round. Maintaining composure after a bad shot is crucial for regaining focus and moving forward. Developing strategies for handling mistakes helps players maintain a positive mindset and stay calm under pressure.

- **Reframe mistakes** – Mistakes should be viewed as opportunities for growth rather than failures. By reframing errors in a positive light, players can quickly recover and refocus on the next shot. Accepting mistakes as part of the game reduces frustration and prevents negative emotions from clouding judgment.

- **Stay positive** – Maintaining a positive attitude throughout the round, even after a mistake, is key to staying composed under pressure. Remind yourself that a single bad shot does not define your performance. Focus on the next opportunity to make a great shot rather than dwelling on past mistakes.

- **Take a break if needed** – If nerves or frustration build up after a mistake or a series of poor shots, it's important to step back and reset. Taking a few moments to breathe, reflect, and regain focus can help players move past a tough stretch and continue with a clear mind.

E. Key Takeaways

Managing nerves and handling pressure are critical skills for performing well in tournaments. Players who can maintain composure in high-stress situations tend to perform better over the course of the event.

- **Understand the source of nerves** – Recognize that nerves are a natural part of competition. Identifying the root cause of your anxiety is the first step to managing it effectively.

- **Breathing and visualization** – Use deep breathing exercises and visualization techniques to stay calm and focused before and during the round.

- **Shift focus to the process** – Focus on executing each shot, rather than stressing over the outcome or score.

- **Handle mistakes with positivity** – View mistakes as learning opportunities and quickly refocus on the next shot.

By using these techniques to manage pressure and tournament nerves, you can stay composed and perform at your best under any circumstances. In the next section, we will explore mental resilience and the development of a strong routine to maintain confidence and focus throughout an entire round.

9.2 Developing Mental Resilience & a Strong Routine

Mental resilience is an essential trait for competitive disc golfers, especially during high-pressure moments when nerves and stress can easily affect performance. Developing mental resilience allows players to stay focused, bounce back from mistakes, and maintain confidence throughout the entire round. Paired with a consistent pre-shot routine, mental resilience can significantly improve your ability to handle adversity and stay in the moment, no matter the circumstances. This section will explore techniques for building mental resilience and establishing a strong, repeatable routine that can help you perform under pressure and improve your overall performance in tournaments.

A solid pre-shot routine builds confidence and keeps you focused under pressure.

A. Understanding Mental Resilience

Mental resilience is the ability to stay composed, bounce back from setbacks, and maintain a positive mindset, even when faced with challenges. In disc golf, this means not letting mistakes, bad rounds, or difficult shots affect your mental state. Resilient players are able to recover quickly from errors, refocus on the next shot, and maintain confidence in their ability to succeed.

- **Emotional regulation** – Mental resilience involves controlling your emotions, especially in response to stress, frustration, or disappointment. By staying calm and composed, resilient players can maintain their focus and perform consistently. Learning how to regulate your emotions is crucial in preventing negativity from affecting your game.

- **Adaptability** – Resilient players are flexible and adaptable, able to adjust to changing circumstances such as bad weather, tough course conditions, or unexpected challenges. Mental resilience involves developing the ability to stay focused and positive, even when things don't go as planned.

- **Growth mindset** – A growth mindset is the belief that abilities can be developed through practice, effort, and learning. Embracing this mindset helps you stay resilient, as you understand that mistakes are part of the learning process and that every setback is an opportunity to improve.

B. Building Mental Resilience

Building mental resilience is a gradual process that requires consistent effort. By adopting strategies such as positive self-talk and focusing on the present, you can improve your ability to remain calm and confident during stressful moments. A resilient mindset helps you recover from setbacks and stay focused on what you can control, which enhances your performance under pressure.

- **Positive self-talk** – Replace negative thoughts with positive affirmations. When you hit a bad shot, don't dwell on it. Instead, remind yourself that you can recover, that mistakes are part of the game, and that you have the skills to perform at your best. Phrases like "I'm capable of making the next shot" or "I've handled this before" can help keep you grounded and confident.

- **Focus on the present** – Mental resilience is all about staying in the present moment. Don't focus on past mistakes or worry about future outcomes. Concentrate on the task at hand, which is executing each shot with precision. The more you can stay focused on the present, the less you'll be affected by nerves and anxiety.

- **Mental rehearsal** – Visualizing success and mentally rehearsing key moments in a tournament can strengthen your ability to perform under pressure. Spend time before and during your round visualizing how you want to handle difficult shots, how you want to feel when you approach the basket, and how you'll stay composed under pressure. This mental practice helps reinforce resilience and prepares you for challenging situations.

- **Practice self-compassion** – Being kind to yourself during tough moments is crucial for building resilience. If you make a mistake, don't be too hard on yourself. Acknowledge the error, learn from it, and move on. Self-compassion helps prevent negative self-talk from undermining your confidence and keeps you focused on improvement.

C. The Importance of a Strong Routine

A strong pre-shot routine is a key component of mental resilience. By creating a repeatable routine, you can develop a sense of consistency and control, which helps reduce anxiety and increase focus. A well-established routine helps you stay calm under pressure and ensures that you're executing each shot with intention, even during high-stakes moments.

- **Creating a pre-shot routine** – Your pre-shot routine should be simple, calming, and focused on the process of making a successful throw. This might include deep breathing, visualizing the shot, and mentally preparing yourself for the next move. The goal is to have a routine that you can perform consistently, regardless of the situation.

- **The routine should be specific** – A strong routine involves specific actions that prepare you for the shot. For example, you might begin by taking a deep breath, followed by a visual check of your surroundings, then a mental rehearsal of your throw. The more specific and detailed your routine is, the more it will help you focus and perform consistently.

- **Consistency is key** – A successful routine requires repetition. By practicing your pre-shot routine consistently, it will become automatic and second nature. When under pressure, a familiar routine will help you maintain focus and calmness, especially in high-stress situations.

- **Staying flexible with the routine** – While consistency is important, it's also necessary to remain flexible. Sometimes, conditions on the course or unexpected challenges may require you to adjust your routine slightly. However, the core elements of your routine should remain constant, providing you with a sense of control no matter the situation.

D. Key Takeaways

Building mental resilience and developing a strong routine are essential for success in disc golf, particularly during high-pressure tournament play.

- **Mental resilience** – Develop emotional regulation, adaptability, and a growth mindset to bounce back from setbacks and stay focused on the present moment.

- **Positive self-talk** – Use affirmations and replace negative thoughts with constructive, empowering statements.

- **Mental rehearsal** – Visualize successful shots and mentally rehearse key moments to prepare for pressure situations.

- **Pre-shot routine** – Establish a simple, repeatable routine that helps you stay calm, focused, and consistent under pressure.

- **Consistency and flexibility** – Practice your routine regularly to make it automatic, but be open to slight adjustments based on the situation.

By strengthening your mental resilience and creating a consistent routine, you'll be better equipped to handle tournament pressure, recover from mistakes, and maintain your confidence throughout the round. In the next chapter, we'll explore how visualization and mental rehearsal can further enhance your performance and prepare you for peak performance on the course.

9.3 Visualization & Mental Rehearsal for Peak Performance

Visualization and mental rehearsal are powerful tools that can significantly improve disc golf performance. These techniques are widely used by professional athletes to enhance skills, increase focus, and prepare mentally for high-stakes situations. By mentally rehearsing key moments and visualizing successful outcomes, players can build confidence, reduce anxiety, and develop a deeper connection with their game. This section explores the importance of visualization and mental rehearsal in disc golf and provides actionable strategies to incorporate these techniques into your routine.

Mental rehearsal primes your mind for success—visualize the shot before you throw.

A. The Power of Visualization

Visualization involves mentally creating vivid images of successful shots and scenarios, allowing players to mentally experience desired outcomes. It prepares you for specific situations and challenges on the course, increasing the likelihood of executing successful shots in real-life play. Visualization helps players reinforce muscle memory, build confidence, and reduce anxiety, especially under competitive conditions.

- **Building muscle memory** – Visualization reinforces muscle memory by mentally practicing the exact motions required for successful throws. When you visualize a shot, you activate the same neural pathways in your brain as when physically performing the action. Over time, this repetition strengthens execution.

- **Increased confidence** – Repeatedly visualizing successful shots builds confidence in your ability to execute them. Focusing on positive outcomes shifts your attention away from mistakes and helps reinforce trust in your skills.

- **Mental rehearsal of key moments** – Visualization isn't only for ideal shots. It also helps prepare for difficult situations, such as a challenging putt or a tricky recovery shot. Mentally rehearsing these moments in advance ensures you stay calm and focused when they arise.

- **Reducing anxiety** – Visualization creates a mental blueprint for handling pressure situations. Seeing yourself succeed in high-pressure moments prepares you to manage stress and stay composed during competition.

B. How to Use Visualization in Disc Golf

Visualization can be applied in various ways during practice and tournament play to enhance performance. By visualizing shots and the entire course layout, players can reduce uncertainty and mentally prepare for challenges. Using visualization consistently before and during a round ensures focus and preparedness.

- **Visualizing each shot** – Before throwing, take a moment to close your eyes and picture the flight path of the disc, its direction, and landing spot. Seeing the ideal outcome in detail reinforces confidence and execution.

- **Course visualization** – Before stepping onto the course, mentally walk through each hole. Imagine how you'll approach each shot, factoring in obstacles and course layout. This reduces uncertainty and helps you feel more prepared.

- **Visualizing your pre-shot routine** – Picture yourself going through your pre-shot process, including breathing exercises, stance, grip, and alignment. Practicing this routine in your mind ensures consistency and focus before each throw.

- **Mental rehearsal for pressure situations** – High-pressure moments, such as a crucial putt or a tight fairway shot, can cause anxiety. Mentally rehearse how you'll handle these moments, imagining yourself staying composed and executing the shot confidently.

C. The Science Behind Visualization

Studies show that visualization has tangible benefits for improving performance. Research on athletes across sports demonstrates that mental rehearsal improves execution, enhances focus, and increases confidence. Visualization activates neural pathways used during real execution, making it easier to perform tasks under pressure.

- **Neural pathways** – Visualization strengthens neural connections by engaging the same pathways used during real execution. This mental practice enhances muscle memory, making it easier to perform consistently under pressure.

- **Confidence and focus** – Athletes who visualize success develop stronger self-belief and reduced anxiety. By picturing yourself excelling, you reinforce positive expectations, helping you maintain a focused, composed mindset in competition.

D. Mental Rehearsal for Tournament Play

Visualization is particularly beneficial in tournament play, where pressure can impact performance. Mental rehearsal prepares players for high-pressure shots and helps them stay composed throughout the round. Visualizing how to handle key moments ensures confidence and a clear mindset when facing tough challenges.

- **Pre-tournament visualization** – Before competing, mentally rehearse the tournament experience. Picture yourself staying focused, executing strong shots, and handling tough situations effectively. This builds confidence and conditions your mind for success.

- **Rehearsing under pressure** – Tournament rounds often include high-pressure shots. Visualizing success in these moments helps players stay focused, calm, and confident when the stakes are high.

- **Coping with mistakes** – Mistakes happen, but mental rehearsal helps you recover quickly. Visualize yourself staying composed after a bad throw or missed putt, refocusing on the next shot with confidence.

E. Creating a Visualization Routine

A consistent visualization routine enhances mental preparedness and game consistency. Regularly practicing visualization before and during a round ensures a strong mental game. Developing this routine helps players remain confident and focused on the course, especially in high-pressure moments.

- **Find a quiet space** – Set aside time before practice or tournaments for focused visualization without distractions.

- **Engage your senses** – Make the visualization as detailed as possible by imagining the sound of chains, the feel of the disc, and the movement of your body.

- **Use slow-motion imagery** – Picture yourself executing each motion slowly and deliberately to reinforce correct mechanics.

- **Repeat regularly** – The more often you visualize, the stronger the mental connection, improving consistency and execution.

F. Integrating Visualization into Daily Practice

To make visualization a habit, incorporate it into your daily disc golf routine. Whether during warm-ups, before key throws, or as part of your mental preparation, consistently reinforcing visualization will lead to better execution. Visualization becomes most effective when it's an automatic part of your pre-round routine.

- **Morning Visualization** – Spend a few minutes each morning visualizing successful rounds, key shots, and positive performances. This sets the tone for confidence and focus throughout the day.

- **Pre-Practice Visualization** – Before every practice session, take a moment to visualize what you want to accomplish. Picture yourself executing each drill successfully and making adjustments when needed.

- **Between Rounds** – Use visualization between tournament rounds to reinforce positive outcomes and correct mistakes from previous rounds. This helps reset your mindset and maintain confidence.

G. Key Takeaways

Visualization and mental rehearsal are essential tools for improving performance and reducing anxiety in competitive disc golf.

- **Mental rehearsal** – Practicing visualization strengthens confidence and enhances muscle memory.

- **Preparation for pressure moments** – Mentally rehearsing difficult shots helps maintain composure under tournament pressure.

- **Scientific benefits** – Visualization strengthens neural pathways, builds confidence, and improves performance by reinforcing positive outcomes.

- **Consistent practice** – Regular visualization training improves focus and execution in both casual rounds and high-stakes competition.

- **Daily application** – Integrating visualization into your routine strengthens mental focus, consistency, and confidence in every aspect of your game.

By integrating visualization into your routine, you'll approach each round with greater focus, confidence, and composure. The next chapter explores strategies for staying calm under pressure, helping you perform at your best in crucial moments.

9.4 Staying Calm After a Bad Throw: Rebounding with Confidence

In any competitive sport, mistakes are inevitable, and disc golf is no exception. Whether it's an errant drive, an inaccurate approach, or a missed putt, a bad throw can cause frustration and anxiety, especially when it comes at a critical moment. However, the ability to rebound from a bad throw with confidence and composure is a key characteristic of successful players. This section focuses on techniques for staying calm after a poor shot, minimizing the impact of mistakes, and maintaining mental resilience throughout the round.

Every player makes mistakes—what matters is how you bounce back.

A. Acknowledging the Mistake Without Dwelling On It

The first step in staying calm after a bad throw is acknowledging the mistake without allowing it to negatively impact the rest of your round. Recognizing that mistakes happen helps players quickly refocus on the next shot rather than dwelling on what went wrong. Dwelling on the mistake not only wastes mental energy but also prevents you from executing the next shot with confidence.

- **Acceptance** – Recognize that no one is perfect, and mistakes are an inevitable part of playing a sport. Accepting the mistake helps prevent frustration from building up and allows you to focus on the next shot. Don't waste time dwelling on the error; instead, refocus on the present and your next steps.

- **Release the mistake** – To let go of a bad throw, take a few seconds to breathe and mentally release the negative emotions attached to it. Visualize the throw in your mind, acknowledge what went wrong, and then mentally move on. Holding onto frustration or regret will only hinder your performance on the next shot.

B. Resetting Your Focus: One Shot at a Time

After a bad throw, it's crucial to reset your focus and take things one shot at a time. Tournament rounds are long, and each hole presents a new challenge, so focusing on the next shot is key to keeping your mental game strong. This process helps prevent mental overload and allows you to stay grounded in the present moment.

- **Focus on the next shot** – Acknowledge the bad throw, but don't let it cloud your judgment for the rest of the round. Instead of thinking about the score or the mistake, focus on your next shot. Break the round down hole by hole, shot by shot. By staying focused on the present task, you eliminate the mental burden caused by past mistakes.

- **Short-term goals** – After a bad throw, set a new short-term goal for the upcoming shot. It could be as simple as executing the shot with better form, hitting the fairway, or making a solid approach to the basket. Having small, attainable goals helps shift your focus away from past errors and keeps you engaged in the game.

- **Positive self-talk** – Using positive self-talk is essential for maintaining confidence after a bad throw. Remind yourself that you are capable of executing a great shot. Phrases like "I've got this" or "I can recover" will help reinforce a positive mindset and keep you from getting bogged down by negative thoughts.

C. Mental Rehearsal for Recovery

Before your next throw, take a moment to mentally rehearse how you will recover from the bad shot. By visualizing yourself making a successful recovery, you mentally prepare for the next phase of your round, which helps to rebuild confidence. This process gives you a clear mental picture of what success looks like moving forward.

- **Visualize a successful recovery shot** – Close your eyes for a moment and imagine yourself making the perfect recovery shot. Visualizing the throw helps create a positive outcome in your mind and builds confidence in your ability to perform. This mental rehearsal reinforces the idea that you can recover from a mistake and regain your focus.

- **Commit to the next shot** – After your mental rehearsal, commit to executing the recovery shot with confidence. Trust your instincts and technique, and focus solely on making the best possible shot moving forward. A positive and decisive mindset is essential for a successful recovery.

D. Developing Emotional Resilience

Building emotional resilience is a key aspect of staying calm and confident after a bad throw. Resilience allows you to recover quickly from mistakes and stay mentally strong throughout the round. The ability to persevere and maintain a positive attitude after a mistake is what separates resilient players from those who struggle under pressure.

- **Stay grounded** – Cultivate emotional resilience by staying grounded in the present moment. Focus on your breathing and remind yourself that you're capable of handling any situation. By staying calm and centered, you'll be able to move forward with a positive mindset and keep your confidence intact.

- **Use mistakes as learning opportunities** – Instead of viewing mistakes as failures, reframe them as opportunities for growth. Every bad throw teaches you something valuable, whether it's a lesson in technique, course management, or mental focus. Use each mistake to improve your game and build resilience for future challenges.

- **Perseverance** – Emotional resilience involves persistence, even when things aren't going your way. Disc golf can be a mentally and physically demanding sport, and bouncing back from setbacks requires a strong sense of perseverance.

Embrace the challenge, and remember that the next shot offers a new opportunity to perform at your best.

E. Key Takeaways

Rebounding from a bad throw is an essential skill for disc golfers, allowing you to maintain your confidence and focus throughout the round.

- **Acknowledge and release** – Accept mistakes as part of the game, and don't dwell on them. Focus on moving forward, not backward.

- **One shot at a time** – Reset your focus after a bad throw by concentrating on the next shot and breaking the round into manageable goals.

- **Positive self-talk** – Reinforce confidence with affirmations that remind you of your ability to recover and succeed.

- **Mental rehearsal** – Visualize yourself making a successful recovery shot to mentally prepare for the next move.

- **Emotional resilience** – Cultivate emotional resilience by staying grounded, learning from mistakes, and persevering through challenges.

By staying calm and focused after a bad throw, you'll be able to recover quickly, maintain your confidence, and perform at your best for the remainder of the round. In the next chapter, we'll explore the mental game in more depth, focusing on how to stay focused and composed throughout the entire tournament.

Chapter 9 Review: The Mental Game – How to Stay Focused & Confident

Chapter 9 focuses on developing the mental strength needed to succeed in disc golf. Managing pressure, staying confident, and maintaining focus are just as important as physical skills, especially in competitive play. A strong mental game helps players stay composed, make smart decisions, and recover quickly from mistakes. Whether competing in tournaments or casual rounds, learning to control emotions, focus on execution, and develop mental resilience can make the difference between an average and outstanding performance.

9.1 Managing Pressure & Tournament Nerves

- **Recognize your nerves** – Nervousness is natural, but how you manage it determines your success. Accepting nerves as part of competition helps prevent them from negatively affecting performance.

- **Breathing exercises** – Deep, controlled breathing helps slow heart rate, reduce tension, and maintain concentration before and during throws.

- **Shift focus** – Instead of worrying about results, concentrate on executing each shot with confidence. Focusing on mechanics rather than outcomes minimizes performance anxiety.

- **Develop a mental checklist** – Establish a pre-shot checklist that includes grip, stance, and release angle to ensure consistency and routine under pressure.

9.2 Developing Mental Resilience & a Strong Routine

- **Positive self-talk** – Replace negative thoughts with confident affirmations to maintain focus and mental stability.

- **Stay in the present** – Letting go of past mistakes and focusing on the next shot is key to maintaining momentum.

- **Mental rehearsal** – Visualizing successful shots reinforces confidence and strengthens muscle memory.

- **Build a consistent routine** – A structured pre-shot routine that includes visualization, deep breathing, and deliberate execution promotes consistency, even under pressure.

9.3 Visualization & Mental Rehearsal for Peak Performance

- **Use mental imagery techniques** – Picture the flight path of the disc from release to landing to improve confidence and accuracy.

- **Rehearse difficult shots** – Visualizing tricky throws before executing them increases preparedness and improves results.

- **Understand the science behind visualization** – Mental imagery activates the same neural pathways as physical practice, improving consistency and execution.

9.4 Staying Calm After a Bad Throw: Rebounding with Confidence

- **Acknowledge mistakes** – Recognizing errors without frustration allows players to move forward without emotional setbacks.

- **Reset focus** – Take a deep breath, clear your mind, and approach the next throw with renewed concentration.

- **Emotional resilience** – Staying positive and composed after a mistake prevents one bad throw from leading to multiple errors.

- **Learn and adjust** – Rather than dwelling on a misfire, analyze what went wrong, make necessary adjustments, and approach the next shot with confidence.

Chapter 9 provides the mental tools needed to stay focused, composed, and resilient in all playing conditions. The next chapter explores advanced strategies for maintaining a competitive mindset and achieving long-term success in disc golf.

Part 4: Expanding Disc Golf Beyond the Basics

This section explores ways to deepen your connection with disc golf by growing the sport, getting involved, and embracing creative play. Whether introducing new players, volunteering, or organizing local events, you'll find actionable steps to help expand disc golf's community. We'll also cover fun variations, including trick shots, glow-in-the-dark night play, and unique course layouts that add excitement to the game. By exploring these new approaches, you'll not only enhance your own enjoyment but also contribute to the sport's growth and accessibility. Whether you're a casual player, competitive athlete, or dedicated organizer, this section will help you discover fresh ways to engage with disc golf, promote its reach, and keep the game fun and dynamic for yourself and others.

Chapter 10: Growing the Sport & Getting Involved

Disc golf thrives through community involvement, and there are many ways to contribute to its growth. This chapter explores how to introduce new players, volunteer for course maintenance, and support local disc golf initiatives. You'll learn how to organize leagues and tournaments, creating opportunities for players of all skill levels to connect and compete. We'll also discuss the future of disc golf, including its global expansion, increasing media presence, and professional growth. Whether you want to promote the sport or deepen your personal involvement, this chapter provides strategies to make a meaningful impact and be part of disc golf's continued rise.

Growing disc golf starts with sharing the sport and welcoming new players.

10.1 How to Introduce New Players to Disc Golf

Introducing new players to disc golf is a rewarding way to grow the sport and share your passion. Disc golf is an accessible, fun, and inclusive activity for people of all ages and skill levels. Whether you're introducing a friend, family member, or a complete newcomer, creating a welcoming and enjoyable experience is key to sparking their interest. This section outlines how to introduce new players to disc golf in a way that ensures they feel confident, informed, and excited to keep playing.

Teaching disc golf to others helps grow the sport for future generations.

A. Keep It Simple and Fun

When introducing someone to disc golf, simplicity is key. Many beginners may not be familiar with the sport, so starting with the basics helps them ease into it without feeling overwhelmed. Keeping things fun and low-pressure makes the learning experience more enjoyable.

- **Explain the basics** – Start with a simple explanation: the goal is to throw the disc into the basket in as few throws as possible. Introduce key terms like "tee pad," "basket," "par," and "hole," but keep explanations brief.

- **Play a casual round** – Instead of focusing on technique or scoring, encourage new players to enjoy throwing the disc and getting a feel for the game. Keeping it relaxed and pressure-free allows them to learn naturally.

- **Encourage teamwork** – If introducing multiple players, try a "best shot" format, where everyone throws and then plays from the best position. This reduces pressure and makes the game more enjoyable.

- **Keep rounds short** – A full 18-hole round can be tiring for beginners. Starting with a shorter round, such as 9 holes or even just a few practice holes, keeps them engaged without becoming overwhelming.

B. Provide the Right Equipment

Having the right equipment can make a big difference in ensuring a smooth and enjoyable introduction to the sport. While professional gear isn't necessary, using beginner-friendly discs and proper footwear enhances the experience.

- **Beginner-friendly discs** – New players should start with a putter and mid-range disc instead of high-speed drivers. These discs provide better control, making it easier to develop proper throwing techniques.

- **Comfortable gear** – Recommend proper footwear, like sneakers or hiking shoes, for comfort on uneven terrain. Also, remind new players to bring water, sunscreen, and appropriate clothing based on the weather.

- **Avoid overwhelming them with gear** – Beginners don't need a bag full of discs. A basic starter set is enough. Once they feel more comfortable, you can introduce them to different disc types and flight patterns.

- **Show them how to grip and throw** – Before starting, take a moment to demonstrate how to grip and release the disc. A basic backhand throw is the easiest place to start, as it's the most commonly used technique.

C. Make It Social and Supportive

One of the best aspects of disc golf is its social nature. A supportive and encouraging environment helps new players feel comfortable, confident, and excited to continue playing.

- **Offer encouragement** – Celebrate small successes and offer positive reinforcement. Even if their throw doesn't go far, acknowledge their effort and improvement.

- **Be patient** – Learning a new sport takes time. Avoid overwhelming new players with too many instructions at once. Let them develop at their own pace and give tips gradually.

- **Help them find their rhythm** – Everyone throws differently. Encourage new players to find a stance and throwing style that feels natural for them rather than forcing them into a specific technique.

- **Encourage group play** – Suggest that new players bring friends or family to make the experience more fun. Playing with others helps them feel like part of a community and keeps them engaged.

D. Introduce Them to the Disc Golf Community

Connecting new players with the larger disc golf community can enhance their experience and keep them engaged. The more they feel involved, the more likely they are to continue playing.

- **Local leagues and tournaments** – After the initial introduction, invite them to local leagues or casual tournaments. These events are beginner-friendly and provide a welcoming environment.

- **Course events and clinics** – Many courses offer beginner clinics where experienced players teach fundamentals. Attending these can help new players improve their skills and feel more confident.

- **Disc golf clubs and meetups** – Encourage them to join local disc golf clubs or community groups. Many clubs host social rounds and events that are great for meeting other players and learning more about the game.

- **Online resources** – Recommend YouTube tutorials, disc golf forums, and social media groups where they can learn techniques, find local events, and connect with other disc golfers.

- **Introduce them to etiquette** – As they get more comfortable, teach them about disc golf etiquette, such as letting faster groups play through, keeping noise levels down when others are throwing, and respecting the course.

E. Fun Drills to Help New Players Improve

For new players, practicing specific skills can help them improve quickly while keeping the experience engaging. Here are a few simple drills that make learning fun:

- **Putting challenge** – Set up a putting challenge where new players try to make putts from different distances. Keep it fun by rewarding successful putts with small prizes or points.

- **Accuracy drills** – Set up targets (such as trees or poles) and have new players practice aiming for them. This helps with accuracy without the pressure of playing full holes.

- **Distance control drill** – Have players throw with half power, then full power, to get a feel for how the disc flies at different speeds. This helps them learn control.

- **Friendly competition** – A little friendly competition can make practice more exciting. Try simple games like "horse" for putting or "closest to the basket" challenges.

F. Key Takeaways

Introducing new players to disc golf is a rewarding experience that helps grow the sport and build community.

- **Keep it simple and fun** – Focus on the basics and make the experience enjoyable with a casual, low-pressure approach.

- **Provide the right equipment** – Use beginner-friendly discs, ensure players have comfortable gear, and keep things simple.

- **Foster a supportive environment** – Encourage new players, be patient, and help them find their throwing style.

- **Connect them with the community** – Introduce new players to leagues, clinics, and online resources to keep them engaged.

- **Make practice fun** – Use putting challenges, accuracy drills, and friendly competition to keep learning exciting.

By following these strategies, you'll not only introduce new players to disc golf but also help them develop a lasting passion for the sport. The next section will explore the importance of volunteering and maintaining courses to give back to the sport you love.

10.2 Volunteering & Course Maintenance: Giving Back to the Community

Volunteering and participating in course maintenance is an excellent way to give back to the disc golf community and contribute to the growth and sustainability of the sport. Whether you're helping out at a local course or working on larger community initiatives, your involvement can make a significant impact. This section will highlight the importance of volunteering, how you can get involved, and how maintaining courses can improve the overall disc golf experience for all players.

Volunteering keeps courses in top shape and strengthens the disc golf community.

A. The Importance of Volunteering in Disc Golf

Volunteering plays a crucial role in the continued growth and development of disc golf as a sport. It fosters a sense of community, ensures that courses remain in good condition, and provides opportunities for players to give back to the sport they love.

- **Supporting the growth of the sport** – Disc golf is a community-driven sport, and volunteering helps strengthen the bonds within that community. By contributing your time and effort, you can help ensure that the sport continues to grow and thrive. Volunteering also increases awareness of the sport, drawing in new players and fans.

- **Enhancing the player experience** – Volunteers play a vital role in maintaining courses, organizing events, and supporting new players. By volunteering, you directly impact the experience of other players, ensuring that they have access to well-maintained courses, fun events, and a welcoming environment to enjoy disc golf.

- **Creating a positive environment** – Volunteering helps cultivate a sense of camaraderie and community in disc golf. When players come together to give back to the sport, it fosters a positive atmosphere and strengthens the relationships between players, clubs, and organizations. This collaboration contributes to the overall success and longevity of the sport.

B. Ways to Volunteer in the Disc Golf Community

There are many ways to get involved and volunteer in the disc golf community. Whether you have a few hours to spare or you're interested in committing to a long-term project, there are plenty of opportunities to make a difference.

- **Course cleanups and maintenance** – Many local disc golf courses rely on volunteers to help with course maintenance. Tasks can range from picking up trash and trimming overgrown areas to repairing baskets and tees. Volunteering for course maintenance ensures that courses remain accessible, safe, and enjoyable for all players. By participating in regular cleanups and improvements, you contribute to the long-term sustainability of the course.

- **Course design and construction** – Some communities offer opportunities for volunteers to assist with the design and construction of new disc golf courses. This may involve site planning, marking fairways, clearing paths, and installing baskets. Participating in course construction allows you to leave a lasting impact on the sport and create new spaces for players to enjoy.

- **Event organization** – Local leagues, tournaments, and clinics often rely on volunteers to help with event planning, registration, scorekeeping, and course setup. Volunteering at events allows you to be part of the excitement and helps ensure that tournaments run smoothly. It's also a great way to meet new people, network with other disc golfers, and make a direct impact on the disc golf scene in your area.

- **Teaching and mentoring** – Many experienced players enjoy mentoring newcomers to the sport. Whether you're running beginner clinics, offering tips at local courses, or helping with youth programs, teaching and mentoring new players is an excellent way to contribute to the sport and help it grow. Sharing your knowledge and passion with others fosters a welcoming environment for new players to enjoy disc golf.

- **Fundraising and advocacy** – Some disc golf clubs and organizations need help raising funds for course improvements or community outreach programs. Fundraising efforts can include organizing charity events, running online campaigns, or hosting raffles. Advocating for disc golf can also involve working with local governments or parks departments to promote course development and protect disc golf spaces.

C. How Course Maintenance Benefits the Community

Course maintenance is essential for ensuring that disc golf courses remain functional, safe, and enjoyable for all players. Well-maintained courses encourage player engagement, attract new players, and improve the overall experience for the community. Here are some key benefits of regular course maintenance:

- **Enhanced playing conditions** – Regular maintenance, such as mowing fairways, clearing paths, and trimming trees, ensures that the course remains playable and safe. A well-maintained course provides players with a better experience, increasing the likelihood that they will return to play and recommend the course to others.

- **Increased safety** – Proper course maintenance also helps address potential safety hazards, such as uneven terrain, overgrown vegetation, or damaged baskets. Ensuring that the course is free of obstacles and hazards minimizes the risk of injury and promotes a safer playing environment for everyone.

- **Attracting new players** – When disc golf courses are well-kept, they are more likely to attract new players. A clean, inviting course signals that the community cares about the sport, encouraging newcomers to give it a try. Well-maintained courses can also increase the visibility of the sport, attracting players from outside the area.

- **Environmental sustainability** – Course maintenance often involves practices that contribute to environmental sustainability. For example, maintaining native vegetation, managing stormwater runoff, and minimizing the use of pesticides can create eco-friendly courses that benefit both the environment and the players. By volunteering for course maintenance, you contribute to a more sustainable disc golf community.

D. Key Takeaways

Volunteering and maintaining courses is a vital part of giving back to the disc golf community and ensuring the sport continues to grow and thrive.

- **Support growth** – Volunteering helps promote the sport, enhances the player experience, and strengthens community bonds.

- **Ways to get involved** – Volunteer for course cleanups, event organization, course construction, teaching, mentoring, or fundraising efforts.

- **Course maintenance benefits** – Regular maintenance improves playing conditions, increases safety, attracts new players, and promotes sustainability.

By getting involved in volunteering and course maintenance, you'll play a key role in the development and success of disc golf in your community. The next section explores creative and alternative ways to play disc golf, offering new and fun challenges to make the sport even more exciting.

10.3 Running Local Leagues & Tournaments: How to Organize Events

Organizing local leagues and tournaments is a great way to engage the disc golf community, grow the sport, and provide competitive opportunities for players of all skill levels. Whether you're setting up a casual league or a high-stakes tournament, proper planning is key to ensuring a smooth and successful event. This section outlines how to organize a disc golf league or tournament, covering planning, promotion, execution, and follow-up.

Organizing events brings disc golfers together and builds a strong local scene.

A. Planning Your League or Tournament

Planning is crucial to the success of any event. Whether it's a casual weekly league or a competitive tournament, mapping out the logistics in advance ensures that everything runs smoothly. The planning process involves making key decisions about the event format, date, location, and other logistics.

- **Choose the format** – Decide if you're hosting a league (a recurring event over weeks or months) or a tournament (a single-day or multi-day competition). Leagues often have a relaxed atmosphere, while tournaments can range from casual to highly competitive.

- **Pick a date and location** – Select a date that doesn't conflict with other local events or major tournaments. Ensure the course is in good condition and has essential amenities such as parking, restrooms, and clear signage.

- **Create divisions** – To make the event fair and inclusive, offer divisions based on skill level, age, or gender. Common divisions include recreational, intermediate, advanced, and pro. Larger tournaments may have separate categories for juniors, women, and senior players.

- **Set an entry fee** – Establish an entry fee that covers event costs like course fees, prizes, and administrative expenses. Keeping it affordable encourages participation, but for larger tournaments, higher fees may be appropriate to fund payouts and sponsorships.

- **Secure necessary permits** – Some parks and public courses require permits for organized events. Check with the park or city officials to ensure you have all the necessary approvals.

B. Promoting Your Event

Promotion is key to attracting participants and creating excitement for the event. Effective promotion will increase attendance and foster community engagement, making your event a success. There are several ways to spread the word and ensure a good turnout.

- **Use social media** – Platforms like Facebook, Instagram, and Twitter are great for advertising events. Create an event page, post updates, and encourage players to invite friends. Use local disc golf groups to spread the word.

- **Partner with businesses** – Local businesses, such as sporting goods stores and coffee shops, can help promote your event in exchange for sponsorship recognition. They may also provide prize donations or discounts for participants.

- **Send email invitations** – If you have an email list, send a detailed invitation with event information, registration details, and reminders leading up to the event.

- **Print flyers** – Posting flyers at disc golf courses, recreation centers, and community bulletin boards can attract local players who may not see online promotions.

- **Word of mouth** – Encourage league members and disc golf clubs to invite friends and spread the word in their local circles.

C. Managing the Event on the Day

On the day of the event, smooth execution is key to providing a great experience for participants. From registration to handling unexpected issues, having a clear plan of action ensures that everything goes according to schedule. Effective management helps create a positive atmosphere for players and volunteers alike.

- **Set up a check-in station** – Have a registration area where players check in, receive scorecards, and get any additional materials, such as course maps or event swag. An online pre-registration system can speed up the check-in process.

- **Organize player groups** – Assign players to groups or cards, either based on skill level, random selection, or pre-seeded rankings. Ensure players understand their starting hole and any special rules for the event.

- **Monitor pace of play** – Assign volunteers to keep track of pace of play and assist if any groups fall behind. For large tournaments, having a course marshal helps ensure rounds move smoothly.

- **Have enough volunteers** – Enlist volunteers to help with registration, scorekeeping, rule enforcement, and logistics. Volunteers make the event more manageable and improve the player experience.

- **Prepare for unexpected issues** – Be ready to handle lost discs, weather delays, or rule disputes. Having a plan for handling these situations ensures the event stays on track.

- **Provide refreshments** – If possible, have water stations or refreshments available, especially for longer events. Hydration and snacks can improve player endurance and enjoyment.

D. Wrapping Up the Event

Once the event concludes, it's important to finish strong by recognizing participants and thanking those who contributed to the success of the event. This helps foster a sense of community and encourages people to participate again in the future.

- **Announce winners and distribute prizes** – Hold an awards ceremony to recognize winners and distribute prizes. Even for non-competitive divisions, consider offering fun awards like "Best Attitude" or "Longest Putt."

- **Thank volunteers and sponsors** – Acknowledge the contributions of volunteers and sponsors, as their support is essential to the event's success.

- **Gather feedback** – Ask participants what they enjoyed and what could be improved. A post-event survey can help refine future tournaments.

- **Post event results** – Share final scores and highlights on social media, email newsletters, or the PDGA website if it's a sanctioned event. Publicizing results keeps players engaged and builds momentum for future events.

- **Plan for future events** – If the event was a success, consider organizing future leagues or tournaments. Regular events build a stronger community, attract new players, and contribute to the overall growth of disc golf in your area.

E. Expanding Your Event for Future Growth

After hosting a successful event, it's time to think about how to expand and improve for future tournaments. Growth requires strategic planning, expanding sponsorships, and offering new formats to keep the community excited.

- **Seek sponsorships** – Partner with larger sponsors to provide funding, player packs, or event swag. Sponsors can help cover costs and add value for participants.

- **Make it a series** – Instead of a single event, create a series of tournaments that lead to a season championship. This encourages players to return and builds long-term interest.

- **Offer new formats** – Experiment with different tournament styles, such as doubles, match play, or glow disc golf. Unique formats attract a variety of players and keep events fresh and exciting.

- **Invest in better infrastructure** – If you plan to host more events, consider investing in scoreboards, tee signs, banners, or custom trophies. These details enhance the professionalism of the event and leave a lasting impression on participants.

F. Key Takeaways

Running local leagues and tournaments is a great way to grow the sport and create a thriving disc golf community.

- **Plan thoroughly** – Define the event format, choose a suitable date and location, and create fair divisions.

- **Promote effectively** – Use social media, local partnerships, and flyers to maximize participation.

- **Manage efficiently** – Have clear check-in procedures, assign groups properly, and ensure smooth pace of play.

- **Wrap up properly** – Announce winners, thank volunteers, and gather feedback to improve future events.

- **Think long-term** – Expand your event, seek sponsorships, and try new formats to keep players engaged.

By following these steps, you can create successful and enjoyable disc golf events that bring players together and strengthen the community. The next section will explore the future of disc golf, including the sport's rapid growth and the increasing role of media and sponsorships in professional play.

10.4 The Future of Disc Golf: Expansion, Media & Professional Growth

The future of disc golf is incredibly exciting, with growth in popularity, professional recognition, and media coverage continually expanding the sport's reach. As more people discover disc golf and the number of players continues to rise, the sport is becoming a more prominent part of the athletic and entertainment landscape. This section will explore the trends and developments that are shaping the future of disc golf, including its expansion into new regions, increasing media presence, and the rise of professional leagues and tournaments.

Disc golf is growing—more courses, bigger tournaments, and increased media coverage.

A. Global Expansion of Disc Golf

Disc golf is rapidly expanding beyond its traditional roots, reaching new players and communities worldwide. The sport's accessibility, low cost, and simple rules have made it a natural fit for global growth. As more countries and communities embrace the sport, the potential for expansion is tremendous.

- **International growth** – Disc golf is gaining popularity in countries around the world, especially in Europe, Asia, and

Oceania. In particular, countries like Finland, Sweden, and Estonia have become hotbeds for the sport, with major tournaments, large disc golf clubs, and a growing number of courses. As the sport's popularity increases globally, more players are discovering the joy of disc golf, contributing to its rapid expansion.

- **New courses worldwide** – With the sport's growth comes the demand for more courses. New courses are being developed in both urban and rural areas, often in parks, forests, and other public spaces. These courses are designed to cater to players of all skill levels, ensuring that disc golf remains inclusive and accessible to everyone.

- **Global tournaments** – Disc golf tournaments are expanding to international venues, with major events like the PDGA World Championships and the European Disc Golf Championships attracting participants from all over the globe. These events showcase the talent and passion for disc golf on an international stage, helping to elevate the sport and its profile.

B. Media Presence & Coverage

The rise of media coverage for disc golf is helping to raise awareness and visibility for the sport, bringing it to new audiences and increasing fan engagement. As disc golf becomes more accessible to the general public, media outlets are beginning to take notice, expanding their coverage of the sport.

- **Televised events** – The increasing media coverage of disc golf has led to televised tournaments, making it easier for fans to follow the sport. Networks like ESPN have aired disc golf events, and YouTube has become a primary platform for live streaming tournaments, with players and organizations broadcasting matches to large audiences. Television coverage helps attract a broader audience, which can inspire new players to try the sport.

- **Social media growth** – Social media platforms have played a significant role in promoting disc golf. Professional players, teams, and organizations regularly use social media to share updates, tutorials, highlights, and behind-the-scenes content. Platforms like Instagram, Facebook, and Twitter allow fans to stay connected to the sport, while YouTube provides a wealth of disc golf content, including tutorials, highlights, and course reviews. As more players and fans engage with social media, the sport's online presence continues to grow.

- **Disc golf-specific media outlets** – As the sport gains momentum, more media outlets dedicated to disc golf are emerging. Websites, podcasts, and blogs that cover news, tips, and event coverage are becoming increasingly popular, allowing fans to stay informed about the latest happenings in the disc golf world. These outlets also provide a platform for discussing the sport's development and connecting the global community.

C. Professional Growth: Leagues, Sponsorships & Player Opportunities

The professional side of disc golf is growing, with more opportunities for players to earn a living from the sport and more sponsorships available for top players. The rise of professional tournaments and the expansion of sponsorships have helped elevate the sport and increase its visibility.

- **Professional leagues** – The Professional Disc Golf Association (PDGA) is the governing body for the sport, overseeing professional leagues and tournaments. The PDGA's involvement has helped create a professional structure for the sport, giving players opportunities to compete at the highest level. The PDGA's pro tour, which includes events like the Disc Golf Pro Tour (DGPT), has become a premier series, attracting top talent and large audiences.

- **Sponsorships** – With the growth of professional disc golf, sponsorships from major brands are becoming more common.

Companies from various industries, such as apparel, beverage, and equipment brands, are recognizing the potential of disc golf and investing in professional players, teams, and events. These sponsorships provide players with the financial backing they need to compete at the highest level, while also helping to raise the sport's profile.

- **Player opportunities** – As professional disc golf continues to grow, more opportunities for players are emerging. The increase in prize money, sponsorships, and media coverage has made disc golf a viable career for top players. Additionally, as the sport gains recognition, players are becoming more prominent in the public eye, providing opportunities for endorsements and other career ventures outside of playing.

- **Youth involvement** – Youth involvement is another crucial element in the future of disc golf. Programs that introduce children to the sport are growing, with schools, community centers, and youth leagues offering disc golf as an extracurricular activity. The younger generation is key to the sport's long-term growth, and getting them involved early will help ensure that disc golf continues to thrive for years to come.

D. Key Takeaways

The future of disc golf is bright, with significant expansion, increasing media coverage, and growing professional opportunities.

- **Global expansion** – Disc golf is growing internationally, with more courses, tournaments, and players around the world.

- **Media coverage** – Television broadcasts, social media platforms, and disc golf-specific outlets are increasing the sport's visibility.

- **Professional growth** – Leagues like the PDGA and sponsorships are providing more opportunities for players to make disc golf a career.

- **Youth involvement** – Introducing younger generations to disc golf ensures the sport's continued growth and longevity.

As disc golf continues to grow and evolve, it offers exciting opportunities for players, organizers, and fans to be part of a rapidly expanding sport. The future of disc golf looks bright, and by contributing to its development, you can help shape the next chapter in its exciting journey. The next chapter will explore the creative side of the sport, with fun ways to mix up the traditional disc golf experience and challenge yourself in new ways.

Chapter 10 Review: Growing the Sport & Getting Involved

Chapter 10 explores how players can contribute to the growth of disc golf and strengthen the community. Whether by introducing new players, maintaining local courses, organizing events, or supporting the sport's expansion, every effort helps disc golf continue to thrive. This chapter highlights ways to make a positive impact, ensuring the sport remains accessible, enjoyable, and sustainable for future generations.

10.1 How to Introduce New Players to Disc Golf

- **Keep it simple and fun** – Focus on enjoyment rather than overwhelming beginners with technique and rules.

- **Provide beginner-friendly equipment** – Loaning out putters or midranges and ensuring players have the right gear enhances their experience.

- **Create a welcoming environment** – Encouraging new players through casual rounds and supportive feedback helps build confidence.

- **Host beginner-friendly events** – Offering free or low-cost clinics introduces more people to the sport in an engaging and structured way.

10.2 Volunteering & Course Maintenance: Giving Back to the Community

- **Participate in course cleanups** – Removing trash, clearing fairways, and repairing tee pads keeps courses playable.

- **Advocate for new courses** – Working with local officials can help bring more disc golf opportunities to communities.

- **Educate on etiquette** – Promoting respect for the course and other players enhances everyone's experience.

- **Build stronger connections** – Volunteering fosters friendships and a sense of community within the sport.

10.3 Running Local Leagues & Tournaments: How to Organize Events

- **Plan event logistics** – Define the format, divisions, and scoring systems to accommodate all skill levels.

- **Promote effectively** – Using social media and local disc golf networks boosts participation.

- **Ensure smooth operations** – Managing tee times, coordinating volunteers, and keeping rounds on schedule improves the event experience.

- **Make events engaging** – Prizes, raffles, and charity-based tournaments add excitement and encourage community involvement.

10.4 The Future of Disc Golf: Expansion, Media & Professional Growth

- **Growing the sport worldwide** – New courses and events are expanding disc golf's reach across different countries.

- **Increased media exposure** – Disc golf's presence on social media and streaming platforms is attracting more fans.

- **Professional opportunities** – Sponsorships and prize money are rising, creating more career paths for elite players.

- **Every player's role** – Whether introducing beginners, maintaining courses, or organizing events, everyone contributes to the sport's continued success.

Chapter 10 highlights how players can get involved and help disc golf grow, from grassroots efforts to professional expansion. The next chapter explores creative and alternative ways to play, keeping the game fresh, exciting, and engaging for all players.

Chapter 11: Creative & Alternative Ways to Play Disc Golf

Finding new ways to play disc golf can add excitement, challenge, and variety to your experience. This chapter explores alternative formats, from trick shots and glow-in-the-dark night golf to safari layouts and unique scoring systems. Whether you're looking to improve your skills, spice up casual rounds, or introduce friendly competition, these variations keep the game fresh and engaging. Playing with different formats fosters adaptability, creativity, and camaraderie among players. By stepping beyond the traditional game, you'll discover new challenges, develop a more versatile skill set, and make every round of disc golf an exciting new adventure.

Disc golf isn't just about competition—explore new ways to challenge yourself and have fun.

11.1 Disc Golf Trick Shots & Creative Challenges

Disc golf trick shots and creative challenges add excitement and variety to the game while improving throwing techniques, adaptability, and overall control. Whether you're playing solo or with friends, these challenges encourage out-of-the-box thinking and push players beyond standard course play. Trick shots test precision and control, while creative challenges foster competition and strategic adjustments. This section explores different trick shot ideas and unique challenges to enhance your skills and bring an element of fun to your disc golf experience.

Trick shots add a fun and inventive twist to your disc golf skills.

A. Trick Shots: Showcasing Creativity & Precision

Trick shots allow players to experiment with different throwing techniques, adding excitement to the game. These challenging shots force players to manipulate disc angles, flight paths, and release points in ways not typically required in regular play. Mastering trick shots boosts creativity and precision in every throw.

- **The Around-the-World Shot** – This shot requires curving the disc around an obstacle, such as a tree or a structure, before landing near the basket. Adjust the release angle and power for success.

- **The No-Look Shot** – This trick challenges players to throw without looking at the target, relying solely on muscle memory, body positioning, and confidence. It's a fun way to test control while adding flair to your game.

- **The Roller Shot** – A disc thrown at an angle that lands on its edge and rolls toward the target. This shot is useful in tight spaces where an airborne throw may be obstructed by trees or other obstacles.

- **The Sky-Anhyzer** – A high-release shot with an exaggerated anhyzer angle, allowing the disc to turn in mid-air before curving back toward the target. This trick is difficult to master but visually impressive when executed correctly.

- **The Behind-the-Back Shot** – A unique and unconventional throw performed by swinging the disc behind the back before release. It enhances coordination and hand-eye control.

- **The Turbo Putt** – A putting technique where the disc is held like a basketball and pushed toward the basket in an overhead motion. This shot is useful when obstacles prevent a normal putting stance.

- **The Thumber & Tomahawk Throws** – These overhand shots send the disc on a vertical flight path before it flips and lands near the target. They're effective for getting over trees or other obstacles in tough situations.

- **The Skip Shot** – This shot involves throwing the disc low to the ground so it skips off a hard surface (such as a dirt path or pavement) toward the target. Mastering this shot can be useful in wooded areas where direct throws are obstructed.

B. Creative Challenges: Thinking Outside the Course

Creative challenges encourage players to modify traditional rules, test new strategies, and develop versatility. These challenges add excitement and unpredictability to casual rounds. They also help players push their limits in a non-competitive environment.

- **Obstacle Course Challenge** – Players navigate a course with additional obstacles like benches and trees. This challenge forces players to adapt and plan unconventional paths.

- **The Distance Challenge** – Each player attempts to achieve the longest drive from a designated spot. This challenge helps refine throwing power and promotes competition.

- **The One-Disc Challenge** – Players complete an entire round using a single disc. Since they must drive, approach, and putt with one disc, this challenge improves adaptability and strategic thinking.

- **The Blindfolded Challenge** – Players attempt to execute throws while blindfolded, relying solely on feel and muscle memory. This challenge tests balance, form, and confidence in throwing mechanics.

- **The Target Challenge** – Specific objects on the course, such as trees or designated landing zones, become bonus targets. Players must hit or land closest to each target using a variety of throws. This enhances precision and creativity.

- **The Wind Challenge** – Play in windy conditions to practice adjusting shot angles, disc selection, and release techniques to handle unpredictable wind gusts effectively.

- **The Left-Handed (or Opposite-Hand) Challenge** – Right-handed players must throw left-handed (or vice versa), improving coordination and forcing them to focus on fundamental throwing mechanics.

- **The Underhand Throw Challenge** – Players must throw all their shots underhand, challenging their ability to adjust angles and control without using their normal throwing motion.

C. Benefits of Trick Shots & Creative Challenges

Engaging in trick shots and creative challenges goes beyond entertainment—they offer real skill-building benefits that translate to overall game improvement. These activities enhance focus, improve muscle memory, and develop versatility. Additionally, they provide a fun way to introduce new players to the sport.

- **Skill Refinement** – Trick shots develop advanced throwing techniques, enhancing overall control, power, and release precision. Creative challenges improve adaptability by forcing players to adjust their strategies to unique situations.

- **Increased Confidence** – Successfully executing trick shots and overcoming challenges boosts confidence. Players who regularly attempt difficult shots learn to handle pressure and approach obstacles with a positive mindset.

- **Enhanced Focus & Coordination** – Many challenges require precise timing, body positioning, and spatial awareness, improving concentration and motor skills over time.

- **Entertainment & Enjoyment** – While trick shots and challenges are a great way to improve your skills, they're also simply fun. They add a new dimension to the game and allow you to enjoy disc golf in a more relaxed and playful way.

- **Social & Competitive Enjoyment** – Trick shots and challenges create friendly rivalries and encourage group participation. They are a great way to introduce beginners to disc golf in a fun and engaging way.

- **Better Adaptability on the Course** – Practicing non-traditional shots can make you a more well-rounded player, giving you an advantage in unexpected situations where standard throws won't work.

- **Developing Shot Creativity** – Players who experiment with creative shots are better equipped to think on their feet during regular play. Learning to manipulate disc angles, flight paths, and obstacles improves overall problem-solving ability on the course.

- **Strengthening Muscle Memory** – Repeating unique throws and challenges conditions the body to handle different types of shots, making players more instinctive and adaptable in competitive play.

D. Key Takeaways

Trick shots and creative challenges offer new ways to enjoy disc golf while improving skills.

- **Trick shots** – Unique throws such as Around-the-World, No-Look, Roller, Sky-Anhyzer, Behind-the-Back, Turbo Putt, Skip Shot, and Overhand Throws provide entertaining and skill-enhancing challenges.

- **Creative challenges** – Modify the game with Obstacle Course, Distance Challenge, One-Disc Challenge, Blindfolded Challenge, Target Challenge, Wind Challenge, Opposite-Hand Challenge, and Underhand Throw to develop strategic thinking.

- **Performance benefits** – These activities refine throwing techniques, increase confidence, enhance focus, strengthen muscle memory, and encourage social engagement.

Incorporating trick shots and challenges into your routine will keep disc golf fresh, fun, and dynamic. The next section will explore exciting variations of the game, including night golf, safari golf, and unique course layouts.

11.2 Playing Night Disc Golf: Glow Discs & Course Setup

Playing disc golf at night offers a completely new and exciting experience, as the sport transitions from daylight to darkness. Night disc golf has grown in popularity thanks to its unique atmosphere, challenge, and the use of glow-in-the-dark discs and course setups. Whether you're looking to spice up your regular rounds or try something completely different, night disc golf offers a fun and engaging twist. This section will explore how to set up a night round, what equipment you'll need, and the safety considerations to keep in mind for a successful night disc golf experience.

Night rounds bring a whole new challenge—glow discs light up the fairways.

A. Essential Equipment for Night Disc Golf

To make the most of your night disc golf experience, you'll need the right equipment to ensure visibility and safety while still enjoying the full challenge of the game. This ensures a smooth, enjoyable round even in low-light conditions.

- **Glow-in-the-dark discs** – The most crucial piece of equipment for night disc golf is the glow-in-the-dark disc. These discs are specifically designed to be visible in low-light conditions, typically equipped with LED lights or reflective materials that glow when charged by light. There are several types of glow discs available, including drivers, midranges, and putters, allowing players to choose the appropriate disc for each shot. Make sure your discs are fully charged before heading out for your round to maximize visibility.

- **Glow sticks and lights** – In addition to glow discs, many players use additional lighting sources to illuminate the course. Glow sticks can be attached to baskets, trees, or posts to mark holes and hazards. LED headlamps are also popular for personal use, allowing players to see their surroundings clearly while keeping their hands free to throw. Some players also use portable LED lights placed around the basket to make the target area more visible from a distance.

- **Reflective course markers** – To help guide players through the course in the dark, it's essential to mark the course and baskets with reflective materials. Adding glow-in-the-dark tape or reflective stickers to tee pads, trees, and baskets makes it easier to navigate, especially when playing on unfamiliar or less well-lit courses. The more lights and markers you add, the more fun and immersive the experience becomes.

- **Bright clothing** – Wearing bright or reflective clothing is a good idea for night disc golf. It ensures that players are visible to each other, especially in groups or tournament settings. Reflective vests or armbands can help keep players safe while navigating the course in low-light conditions.

B. Course Setup and Layout for Night Disc Golf

Setting up a course for night play requires a bit more thought than a traditional daylight round, as visibility and safety are critical. Here are a few tips for setting up a night disc golf course to ensure a smooth, enjoyable round.

- **Strategic lighting placement** – Place lights and glow markers around the course in key areas, including tees, baskets, and hazards. The baskets should be illuminated from various angles to make them visible from all parts of the fairway. The goal is to create a well-lit path that helps players navigate the course safely without compromising the challenge.

- **Choose a well-defined course layout** – If you're setting up a temporary night disc golf course, pick a layout with clear fairways and limited obstacles. Avoid courses with dense trees or excessive foliage, as they may be difficult to navigate in the dark. Open, less obstructed areas allow players to focus on their throws and enjoy the experience.

- **Set up designated lighting zones** – For safety, ensure that the course has clearly defined zones for lights. You can set up lighted areas for tee pads, fairways, and baskets while keeping any out-of-bounds or hazard areas dark to maintain the challenge of the game. It's important to avoid over-illuminating the course, as too much light can take away from the night-time atmosphere.

- **Create a glowing target zone** – Make sure the baskets are lit clearly to ensure visibility and make it easier for players to line up their putts. You can wrap the basket with string lights, place a light at the top of the basket, or hang glow sticks around it. A well-lit basket creates an exciting target for players while adding to the thrill of night play.

C. Safety Considerations for Night Disc Golf

While night disc golf can be incredibly fun, it's important to keep safety in mind. Playing in the dark presents unique challenges, but with the proper precautions, it can be an enjoyable and safe experience for all players involved.

- **Stay visible** – Always wear reflective or brightly colored clothing to make sure you can be easily seen by other players, especially in group play. It's also essential to use lights and markers around the course to guide players to different holes and avoid collisions.

- **Be aware of your surroundings** – With limited visibility, players should stay aware of any hazards or obstacles that could cause injury. This includes uneven terrain, trees, and low-hanging branches. Always be cautious while walking or throwing in the dark, and make sure the course has adequate lighting in key areas like tees and baskets.

- **Travel in groups** – Playing in groups is recommended for safety reasons. Not only does it make the experience more enjoyable, but traveling in groups also ensures that if something goes wrong, help is readily available. Disc golf can take you into areas with little natural light, so having multiple players on the course adds an extra layer of safety.

- **Consider weather conditions** – Nighttime temperatures can be significantly colder than daytime, so it's important to dress appropriately for the weather. Make sure you and your group are prepared for the conditions, whether it's chilly or rainy, by wearing layers and bringing extra gear if needed.

D. Key Takeaways

Night disc golf offers a thrilling new way to experience the sport, with unique challenges and exciting atmosphere.

- **Glow-in-the-dark discs** – These are essential for playing at night and provide the visibility needed to throw accurately.

- **Course setup** – Use strategically placed lights and glow markers to illuminate the course, making it easier to navigate and more exciting.

- **Safety first** – Ensure you stay visible with reflective clothing, and be cautious of your surroundings when navigating the course in low light.

By preparing with the right equipment and being mindful of safety, you can enjoy the thrill of playing disc golf under the stars. The next section will explore alternative ways to play the game, such as Safari Golf and creative variations that add excitement to your disc golf experience.

11.3 Safari Golf: Creating Custom Holes & Unique Layouts

Safari Golf is an exciting way to reimagine disc golf by designing custom holes and layouts, using natural features and obstacles to create unique challenges. This variation encourages creativity, problem-solving, and skill development, allowing players to explore new ways to navigate a course. Whether you're looking to add variety to your local course or engage in friendly competition, Safari Golf offers an exciting alternative that keeps the game fresh and dynamic. This section will cover the fundamentals of Safari Golf, how to set up your own custom course, and the benefits of playing with unique layouts.

Safari golf allows you to get creative—design your own course and test new layouts.

A. What is Safari Golf?

Safari Golf is an informal variation of disc golf where players design their own holes, creating an unpredictable and customized experience. Instead of following a set course layout, players establish their own tee locations, target areas, and obstacles, adding an element of spontaneity and creativity to the game. This allows players to challenge themselves in a completely new way, using the natural environment to shape the round.

- **Customized holes** – Players choose where each hole begins and ends, modifying traditional courses or setting up a new layout from scratch. Trees, water, elevation, and man-made structures can be incorporated to shape each hole.

- **No fixed rules** – Unlike standard disc golf, Safari Golf allows for complete flexibility in course design and rules. Players can introduce creative challenges, adjust par settings, and modify obstacles to suit their skill levels and preferences.

New perspectives on familiar courses – Safari Golf allows
players see their favorite courses in a fresh way,
playing layouts that challenge shot selection, accuracy,
reintability.

et Up a Safari Golf Course

B. afari Golf course is simple and customizable. Players can
t and technical holes or long and challenging layouts
on the terrain and level of difficulty they want to introduce.
bility makes it an ideal option for creating a unique and
g experience every time.

Choose the location – Safari Golf can be played on an
existing disc golf course, an open park, or a natural setting.
Ideal locations include courses with diverse landscapes, trees,
elevation changes, and open fairways to allow for creative
shot-making.

- **Select tee and target locations** – The flexibility of Safari Golf
  means players can choose unconventional starting points and
  targets. Instead of using traditional tee pads, players can start
  from hills, clearings, or designated areas. Targets can include
  disc golf baskets, trees, benches, or even specific landing
  zones.

- **Incorporate natural obstacles** – One of the best aspects of
  Safari Golf is utilizing the environment to make shots more
  interesting. Trees, water hazards, boulders, fences, and
  elevation changes can all be incorporated to create creative
  shot paths and unique challenges.

- **Establish boundaries and mandatories** – Players can add
  out-of-bounds areas or "mandatories" (mandos) that require
  throws to pass specific landmarks or follow designated routes.
  This ensures the game remains challenging and encourages
  strategic shot selection.

- **Vary par settings** – Custom courses can include holes of
  varying difficulty, with players deciding the par for each hole

based on its length and obstacles. Some hol~~ may require precise technical shots, while others can emphy~~ ~~distance~~ and power.

C. Fun Safari Golf Challenges

Safari Golf is a great opportunity to experiment with new way~~ play. By adding challenges to the custom holes, players can furt~~ enhance their skill-building experience while having fun. Here are some creative variations that can be used to spice up a Safari Golf round.

- **Longest Hole Challenge** – Players design an extra-long hole that spans across multiple fairways, forcing competitors to use power and accuracy to reach the target.

- **Tight Gap Challenge** – Create a hole that requires throwing through a narrow gap, testing precision and control.

- **Elevation Challenge** – Set up a hole that starts from an elevated position, requiring players to navigate a downhill throw or throw uphill toward a challenging target.

- **Blind Shot Challenge** – Players set up a hole where they cannot see the target from the tee area, forcing them to rely on skill and memory to land the disc in an ideal spot.

- **Water Hazard Challenge** – Players incorporate a creek, pond, or designated "hazard" area into the layout, forcing strategic shot selection to avoid penalty strokes.

- **Opposite-Hand Challenge** – To test versatility, players must throw with their non-dominant hand for an entire hole, emphasizing control and adaptability.

- **Overhand-Only Challenge** – Every shot must be thrown using an overhand throw, such as a tomahawk or thumber, requiring players to master a different release angle and disc flight path.

D. Benefits of Safari Golf

Safari Golf offers numerous benefits beyond just having fun. This unique variation of the game improves skills, promotes creativity, and enhances the overall enjoyment of disc golf. By stepping outside the usual course design, players develop new abilities and experience the game from a fresh perspective.

- **Enhanced shot-making skills** – Playing unfamiliar holes encourages players to expand their throwing techniques, making them more adaptable and well-rounded.

- **Increased creativity** – Designing custom holes fosters creativity by challenging players to think outside the box and come up with unique ways to navigate obstacles.

- **More variety in gameplay** – Standard courses can become repetitive, but Safari Golf keeps rounds fresh and engaging by offering new challenges and unpredictable layouts.

- **Improved strategic thinking** – Since each hole is different, players must analyze and plan their shots more carefully, refining decision-making skills on the course.

- **Great for group play** – Safari Golf is ideal for casual rounds with friends or family, encouraging social interaction, teamwork, and friendly competition.

- **Adaptability for all skill levels** – Players can modify holes to match their skill levels, making it a great option for introducing beginners to disc golf while also challenging more advanced players.

E. Key Takeaways

Safari Golf transforms traditional disc golf by allowing players to design their own holes, creating exciting and unpredictable challenges. By using natural obstacles and creativity, players can experience the game in a whole new way.

- **Custom holes and layouts** – Players select their own tee and target locations, incorporating natural features and obstacles for added difficulty.

- **Creative course variations** – Challenges like Longest Hole, Tight Gap, and Water Hazard add excitement and skill development.

- **Skill-building benefits** – Playing Safari Golf improves shot selection, creativity, adaptability, and strategic thinking.

- **Social and competitive enjoyment** – This format is perfect for engaging with friends, making casual rounds more exciting and dynamic.

By incorporating Safari Golf into your disc golf routine, you'll experience the game in a fresh and entertaining way. The next section will explore additional disc golf variations, including team-based formats and unique game styles that add even more diversity to your play.

11.4 Disc Golf Games: Doubles, Match Play & Fun Variations

Disc golf is a dynamic sport that offers a variety of game formats beyond traditional stroke play. Exploring different game types can add excitement, promote strategy, and provide new challenges to improve skills. Whether you enjoy team-based formats like doubles, head-to-head competition in match play, or unique twists that test creativity, there are many ways to make your rounds more engaging. This section explores some of the most popular alternative disc golf formats, including doubles, match play, and other fun variations.

Doubles, match play, and alternative formats keep disc golf exciting and competitive.

A. Doubles Disc Golf: Team Play for Fun & Strategy

Doubles disc golf is a team-based format where two players work together to complete each hole. It enhances strategy, teamwork, and adaptability, making it a great format for casual and competitive play. Different versions of doubles create unique challenges, requiring players to plan their shots carefully and complement each other's strengths.

- **Best Shot Doubles** – Both players throw from the tee, and the team selects the best throw to play from. This continues until the hole is completed. Best Shot allows teammates to compensate for each other's weaknesses, making it ideal for all skill levels.

- **Alternate Shot Doubles** – Players take turns throwing each shot, alternating until the hole is finished. This format requires trust and communication, as teammates rely on each other's consistency to perform well.

- **Worst Shot Doubles** – The opposite of Best Shot, the team must play from the worst of their two throws. This makes for a tough but fun challenge, forcing teams to recover from difficult positions.

- **Modified Doubles** – Some tournaments introduce modified rules, such as limiting disc selections or requiring both players to tee off a set number of times. These variations keep the format fresh and add an extra layer of strategy.

B. Match Play: Head-to-Head Competition

Match play is a format where players compete hole by hole rather than counting total strokes. It allows for aggressive play, as each hole is a separate contest, meaning a bad hole won't ruin an entire round. The format fosters exciting comebacks and encourages players to take calculated risks.

- **Basic Rules** – The player (or team) with the lowest score on a hole wins that hole. If both players tie, the hole is "halved." The match winner is the player who wins the most holes.

- **Strategic Play** – Since only individual holes matter, players can be more aggressive with riskier shots, knowing that a bad hole won't affect the entire round.

- **Handicap Match Play** – Higher-skilled players may give strokes to their opponent to level the playing field, making it more competitive for all skill levels.

- **Best-of Format** – Some match play events require players to win a certain number of holes rather than playing all 18, adding an extra level of suspense.

C. Fun Disc Golf Variations: Adding New Challenges

Creative disc golf formats add variety and introduce unique ways to approach a round. These variations help players improve different skills while making the game more fun and engaging. Whether it's using a single disc, playing under time constraints, or creating custom holes, these formats encourage adaptability and fresh gameplay experiences.

- **One-Disc Challenge** – Players must use a single disc for the entire round, forcing them to adapt and make a variety of throws with just one tool.

- **Tee-to-Basket Challenge** – Players start from unique or extended tee locations, requiring long throws and precise approaches to reach the basket.

- **Worst Shot Singles** – Similar to Worst Shot Doubles but played individually. Players throw twice per turn and must continue from their worse throw, emphasizing consistency and recovery skills.

- **Ring of Fire** – A putting game often played after rounds or during events. All players stand in a circle around the basket and putt at the same time. The last player to miss is eliminated until a winner remains.

- **Speed Golf** – Players attempt to complete the course as quickly as possible, running between shots while maintaining accuracy. This adds a fitness element to the game.

- **Disc Limit Challenge** – Players are restricted to using only a set number of discs, such as three for an entire round. This forces strategic decision-making on disc selection.

- **Odd-Throw Challenge** – Players must alternate between specific throws (e.g., backhand on odd-numbered holes, forehand on even-numbered holes), improving versatility.

- **Safari Golf** – Players design custom course layouts using existing baskets but selecting alternative tee locations, creating a fresh and challenging experience.

D. Benefits of Alternative Disc Golf Formats

Alternative disc golf formats help players develop skills, improve decision-making, and keep the game fresh. Trying different formats enhances adaptability while making rounds more fun and interactive. Many formats also encourage teamwork and social play, helping players of all skill levels enjoy the game.

- **Skill Development** – Different formats challenge players in unique ways, from putting under pressure to recovering from bad lies.

- **Strategic Thinking** – Formats like match play and alternate shot doubles encourage players to think ahead and make smart shot selections.

- **Social & Team Play** – Many formats promote collaboration and friendly competition, making disc golf more accessible and engaging for everyone.

- **Breaking Routine** – Playing the same course in the same way can become repetitive. Alternative formats keep rounds fresh and exciting.

- **Inclusivity** – Some formats, such as Best Shot Doubles or Handicap Match Play, allow players of different skill levels to compete together on a fair and enjoyable playing field.

E. Key Takeaways

Exploring alternative disc golf formats adds variety, strategy, and enjoyment to the game.

- **Doubles disc golf** – Best Shot, Alternate Shot, and Worst Shot encourage teamwork while adding a fun and strategic element.

- **Match play** – A competitive, hole-by-hole format that encourages risk-taking and direct competition.

- **Creative variations** – Games like the One-Disc Challenge, Safari Golf, and Speed Golf introduce fresh challenges that develop new skills and keep rounds interesting.

- **Skill-building and engagement** – Alternative formats improve adaptability, encourage social interaction, and make the game more enjoyable for all skill levels.

By incorporating these different formats into your disc golf routine, you'll discover fresh ways to challenge yourself, connect with other players, and enhance your overall enjoyment of the sport. The next section will explore the growing influence of disc golf in media, professional events, and the future of the sport.

Chapter 11 Review: Creative & Alternative Ways to Play Disc Golf

Chapter 11 explored a variety of creative and alternative ways to enjoy disc golf, offering exciting challenges that add fun and variety to the game. Whether you want to experiment with trick shots, play at night with glow-in-the-dark discs, or design your own custom holes, these variations keep the game fresh and engaging. Trying new formats helps players develop different skills while keeping rounds exciting, social, and unpredictable.

11.1 Disc Golf Trick Shots & Creative Challenges

- **Trick shots** – Experimenting with shots like the Around-the-World, No-Look, and Roller Shot improves creativity and control.

- **Creative challenges** – Setting up obstacle courses, using mandatories, or trying Blindfolded Disc Golf tests adaptability and strategic thinking.

- **Playing with new limitations** – Throwing with non-dominant hands or only using a putter for an entire round forces players to refine different aspects of their game.

11.2 Playing Night Disc Golf: Glow Discs & Course Setup

- **Glow-in-the-dark discs** – Special glow plastic or LED-lit discs allow for night play, adding a new challenge to shot execution.

- **Course setup** – Using glow sticks, reflective tape, or portable LED markers ensures visibility and safety during nighttime rounds.

- **Adjusting for darkness** – Players rely more on feel, flight memory, and controlled throws, which improves precision and touch.

11.3 Safari Golf: Creating Custom Holes & Unique Layouts

- **Customized layouts** – Safari Golf lets players create extended holes, mix different baskets and tees, or incorporate natural obstacles.

- **Using the environment** – Hills, trees, and water features add creativity to hole design, testing strategic shot-making.

- **Skill-building through variety** – Playing new hole designs improves adaptability and helps players develop a wider range of shots.

11.4 Disc Golf Games: Doubles, Match Play & Fun Variations

- **Doubles formats** – Best Shot and Alternate Shot Doubles emphasize teamwork, making the game more interactive and strategic.

- **Match play** – Competing hole-by-hole instead of stroke totals shifts the focus to strategy rather than overall score.

- **Unique variations** – Games like One-Disc Challenge, Speed Disc Golf, and Random Club Selection provide entertaining, skill-testing formats.

Chapter 11 introduced a variety of creative ways to enjoy disc golf, from custom challenges and trick shots to fun new formats. These variations not only make the game more exciting but also refine skills in different scenarios. As we move into the conclusion, we'll reflect on the journey of disc golf, key takeaways from the book, and how players can continue improving and enjoying the sport for years to come.

Conclusion

HowExpert Guide to Disc Golf has taken you through every aspect of the game, from learning the fundamentals to refining advanced strategies and competing at higher levels. Disc golf is more than just a sport—it's a lifelong journey of growth, challenge, and enjoyment. Whether you started as a casual player or are striving for competitive success, disc golf offers endless opportunities to improve your skills, challenge yourself, and experience the thrill of the game. Now, it's up to you to take what you've learned and apply it on the course.

The disc golf journey never ends—keep playing, improving, and enjoying every round.

I. Final Thoughts on the Journey of Disc Golf

Disc golf is unique because it is accessible to players of all ages and skill levels, yet it presents an exciting challenge that keeps you coming back for more. Every round is an opportunity to refine your technique, test your mental toughness, and adapt to the course conditions. Whether you're playing in a quiet park, competing in a high-stakes tournament, or introducing a friend to the sport, each throw helps shape your journey.

The true beauty of disc golf is that it is a sport that evolves with you. As you improve, your understanding of the game deepens—what once seemed difficult becomes second nature, and new challenges emerge to keep you motivated. Every fairway, every basket, and every shot presents a chance to grow as a player.

II. How to Keep Improving & Enjoying the Sport

Like any skill, disc golf improvement comes with consistent effort, smart practice, and a passion for learning. Here are a few key ways to keep advancing your game while maintaining the fun and excitement of the sport:

- **Play a variety of courses** – Exposure to different layouts, elevations, and hazards will develop your shot selection and adaptability.

- **Record and analyze your throws** – Watching yourself play can reveal areas where you can improve, from grip to follow-through.

- **Develop a structured practice routine** – Dedicate time to putting, midrange shots, and drives to refine different aspects of your game.

- **Compete in tournaments or leagues** – Testing yourself against others helps build confidence and experience in high-pressure situations.

- **Engage with the disc golf community** – Learning from experienced players, watching professional tournaments, and staying involved in local disc golf events can provide valuable insights.

Above all, remember to keep disc golf fun. Try new shots, play relaxed rounds with friends, and celebrate small improvements. Whether you're playing for recreation or competition, disc golf should always be an enjoyable and rewarding experience.

III. Next Steps: From Casual Play to Competitive Success

No matter your current level, there is always a next step in your disc golf journey. If you're a casual player, you might set personal goals to lower your scores, hit longer drives, or make more consistent putts. If you have a competitive mindset, you may want to start entering tournaments, mastering mental strategies, and fine-tuning your shot selection under pressure.

For those looking to make a greater impact, consider giving back to the sport. Introduce new players to the game, volunteer for course maintenance, or even organize local disc golf events. The growth of disc golf depends on passionate players who love the game and share it with others.

HowExpert Guide to Disc Golf has given you the knowledge and tools to elevate your game. Now it's time to take action. Whether you're aiming for personal milestones, competitive achievements, or just more unforgettable moments on the course, disc golf is waiting for you.

So grab your discs, step up to the tee, and embrace the next challenge—one throw at a time.

Appendices

The appendices serve as a valuable reference section to enhance your disc golf knowledge, equip you with the best tools, and connect you with the larger disc golf community. Whether you're looking to refine your terminology, invest in the right gear, discover top-tier courses, or access expert training resources, this section provides essential information to support your growth in the sport. From understanding key disc golf terms to finding must-play courses and trusted sources for improving your skills, these appendices ensure you have everything you need to continue your journey—on and off the course.

Master every aspect of disc golf—from rules and gear to world-class courses and expert training.

Appendix A: Disc Golf Glossary from A to Z

Understanding the language of disc golf is essential for improving your game and communicating effectively with other players. This glossary covers key disc golf terms from A to Z, helping you navigate everything from throwing techniques to course rules and tournament play.

Master the language of disc golf with this comprehensive glossary.

A

- **Ace** – A hole-in-one in disc golf, where the disc lands in the basket on the first throw.

- **Anhyzer** – A throwing angle where the disc is released with the outer edge tilted downward, causing it to curve opposite of its natural flight path.

- **Approach Shot** – A throw intended to land close to the basket, setting up an easy putt.

B

- **Backhand** – A common throwing style where the disc is released with the back of the hand facing the target.

- **Basket** – The metal target consisting of a pole, chains, and a catching tray where players aim to land their disc.

- **Bead** – A ridge on the bottom edge of a disc, often found on putters for added grip and stability.

- **Birdie** – Completing a hole in one stroke under par.

- **Bogey** – Completing a hole in one stroke over par.

- **Break In** – The process of wearing in a disc, altering its flight characteristics over time.

C

- **C1 (Circle 1)** – The area within 10 meters (33 feet) of the basket where jump putts and step putts are not allowed.

- **C2 (Circle 2)** – The area between 10 and 20 meters (33–66 feet) from the basket, where step putts and jump putts are allowed.

- **Card** – A group of players who play a round together and track each other's scores.

- **Chains** – The hanging metal links on a disc golf basket that help catch the disc.

- **Chucker** – A casual or reckless player who disregards course etiquette.
- **Course** – A designated disc golf layout consisting of multiple holes.

D

- **Dead Disc** – A disc that has stopped moving and is no longer in play.
- **Drive** – A long-distance throw, typically made from the tee pad.
- **Drop Zone** – A designated area where a player must throw after an out-of-bounds or penalty situation.
- **Dyeing** – The process of applying custom artwork to a disc.

E

- **Eagle** – Completing a hole two strokes under par.
- **Elevated Basket** – A basket placed on a raised surface or structure to add difficulty.
- **Escape Shot** – A throw used to recover from an obstructed lie, such as in thick woods.

F

- **Fade** – The natural tendency of a disc to curve left (for a right-hand backhand throw) at the end of its flight.
- **Fairway** – The main playing area between the tee and the basket.
- **Fairway Driver** – A disc with moderate speed and glide, typically used for controlled distance shots.
- **Flex Shot** – A shot that begins with an anhyzer angle but flexes back in the opposite direction due to disc stability.
- **Flight Numbers** – A four-number system (speed, glide, turn, fade) used to describe how a disc is expected to fly.

- **Forehand (Flick)** – A throwing style where the disc is released with the palm facing the target.

G

- **Grip Lock** – A throwing mistake where the disc is held too long, causing it to release late and veer off course.

- **Gimme** – A short putt that is almost guaranteed to go in.

- **Glide** – The second flight number that measures how well a disc maintains loft and stays in the air.

H

- **Heiser Bomb** – A high-arcing hyzer shot designed to spike into the ground near the target.

- **Hole** – A single playing unit in disc golf, consisting of a tee area, fairway, and basket.

- **Hyzer** – A throwing angle where the outer edge of the disc is tilted upward, causing the disc to curve along its natural flight path.

I

- **Island Hole** – A hole with a designated in-bounds landing area, often surrounded by out-of-bounds (OB) zones.

- **Inside the Circle** – The area within 10 meters (33 feet) of the basket where players must maintain balance while putting.

J

- **Jump Putt** – A putting technique where a player jumps forward while releasing the disc to generate extra power (only legal outside Circle 1).

K

- **Kick** – When a disc unexpectedly bounces off a tree or obstacle, often altering its intended path.

L

- **Layup** – A safe, controlled throw designed to land near the basket rather than attempting an aggressive putt.

- **Lie** – The position where the disc lands and from which the next throw must be taken.

M

- **Mandos (Mandatory Routes)** – Course-designated areas where a disc must pass to avoid penalties.

- **Marker Disc** – A mini disc used to mark a player's lie before throwing.

- **Midrange Disc** – A disc designed for medium-distance, controlled throws.

N

- **Noodle Arm** – A term for a player with low throwing power.

- **No Look Putt** – A putting technique where the player releases the disc without directly aiming at the basket.

O

- **OB (Out of Bounds)** – A designated area where a disc is not allowed to land, resulting in a penalty stroke.

- **Overstable** – A disc that curves more sharply to the left (for right-hand backhand throws) due to high stability.

P

- **Par** – The expected number of throws needed to complete a hole.

- **Penalty Stroke** – An extra stroke added to a player's score due to a rule violation.

- **Power Grip** – A grip style used to maximize distance when throwing drives.

- **Putt** – A short throw intended to land the disc in the basket.

Q

- **Quiet Course** – A course with fewer players, offering a relaxed, slower-paced round.

R

- **Roller** – A throw where the disc lands on its edge and rolls forward instead of flying through the air.

- **Rough** – Dense vegetation or difficult terrain surrounding the fairway.

S

- **Sandbagger** – A player who competes in a lower division than their skill level to gain an advantage.

- **Sidearm (Forehand)** – Another term for the flick throw.

- **Skip Shot** – A throw that intentionally skips off the ground to reach the target.

T

- **Tee Pad** – The designated area from which players throw their first shot on a hole.

- **Turn** – The third flight number that describes how much a disc curves to the right (for a right-hand backhand throw) during its flight.

U

- **Understable** – A disc that turns more to the right (for a right-hand backhand throw) when thrown at high speeds.

- **Upshot** – Another term for an approach shot.

V

- **Vertical Release Angle** – The angle at which a disc is released, affecting its flight path.

W

- **Wind Read** – The skill of analyzing wind conditions and adjusting throws accordingly.

X

- **X-Step** – A common footwork technique used to generate momentum during a drive.

Y

- **Yaw** – The side-to-side movement of a disc in flight, affecting its stability and flight path.

Z

- **Zero Glide** – A term for discs with minimal lift, used for controlled shots.

~ ~ ~ ~ ~

This glossary ensures you're equipped with the language of disc golf, helping you communicate with players, improve your game, and enhance your understanding of the sport.

Appendix B: Recommended Gear & Brands

Having the right gear can make a significant difference in your disc golf experience, whether you're just starting or competing at an advanced level. From high-quality discs to essential accessories, choosing the best equipment helps maximize your performance, consistency, and enjoyment on the course. This section covers some of the top disc golf brands and must-have gear, providing guidance on selecting the right discs, bags, and other essentials for players of all skill levels.

Find the best gear for your game with recommendations from top manufacturers.

I. Top Disc Golf Manufacturers

Disc golf brands vary in terms of disc molds, plastic types, and flight characteristics. Here are some of the top manufacturers known for their quality and reliability:

1. Innova - www.innovadiscs.com

One of the most recognized brands in disc golf, Innova offers a wide range of discs suitable for all skill levels. Their lineup includes the **Destroyer (Distance Driver)**, **Roc (Midrange)**, and **Aviar (Putter)**.

2. Discraft - www.discraft.com

Known for producing high-quality discs with consistent flight characteristics, Discraft is another industry leader. Popular models include the **Buzzz (Midrange)**, **Nuke (Distance Driver)**, and **Luna (Putter)**. Discraft is also the preferred brand of professional players like Paul McBeth.

3. Dynamic Discs - www.dynamicdiscs.com

A favorite among players for their well-balanced discs and premium plastics, Dynamic Discs has gained a strong following. Notable discs include the **Judge (Putter)**, **Trespass (Distance Driver)**, and **Emac Truth (Midrange)**.

4. Latitude 64 - www.latitude64.se

Based in Sweden, Latitude 64 is known for its high-quality plastics and innovative designs. Popular discs include the **Pure (Putter)**, **River (Fairway Driver)**, and **Ballista Pro (Distance Driver)**.

5. MVP Disc Sports - www.mvpdiscsports.com

MVP is recognized for its unique gyro technology, which enhances the stability and glide of their discs. Some of their best-known discs are the **Tesla (Distance Driver)**, **Atom (Putter)**, and **Hex (Midrange)**.

6. Axiom Discs - www.axiomdiscs.com

A sub-brand of MVP, Axiom is known for vibrant colors and visually appealing designs while maintaining MVP's gyro technology. Popular models include the **Envy (Putter)** and **Insanity (Distance Driver)**.

7. Prodigy Discs - www.prodigydisc.com

Prodigy introduced a unique naming system (A, B, C for putters, and 1, 2, 3 for drivers). Some of their standout discs include the **PA-3 (Putter)**, **F3 (Fairway Driver)**, and **D2 (Distance Driver)**.

8. Westside Discs - www.westsidediscs.com

Part of the Trilogy lineup with Latitude 64 and Dynamic Discs, Westside is known for unique disc names and high-quality plastics. Key discs include the **Harp (Overstable Putter)**, **Sword (Distance Driver)**, and **King (Maximum Distance Driver)**.

9. Kastaplast - www.kastaplast.se

A smaller but growing brand, Kastaplast is known for premium plastics and Scandinavian quality. Popular choices include the **Berg (Putter)** and **Lots (Fairway Driver)**.

10. Thought Space Athletics - www.thoughtspaceathletics.com

This brand focuses on artistic designs and unique disc molds. Some of their most sought-after discs include the **Mantra (Control Driver)** and **Synapse (Distance Driver)**.

II. Essential Disc Golf Gear & Accessories

Beyond discs, having the right accessories can improve both your performance and comfort on the course. From high-quality bags and markers to towels and retrievers, having the right gear ensures you're prepared for any situation.

1. Disc Golf Bags & Backpacks

A comfortable and well-organized bag can improve your playing experience by making it easy to carry multiple discs and accessories.

- **Beginner-Friendly Bags** – Compact and affordable options like the **Innova Starter Bag** or **Dynamic Discs Trooper** are great for casual players.

- **Mid-Range Backpacks** – If you carry 15–20 discs, consider the **Grip EQ BX3** or **Upper Park Shift** for extra storage and comfort.

- **Professional-Grade Bags** – For serious players, the **Grip EQ AX5** and **Pound Octothorpe** provide top-tier durability, capacity, and comfort.

2. Mini Markers

Mini markers are used to mark a player's lie before throwing. Brands like **Zing Mini Discs** and **Dynamic Discs Mini Judges** are great options.

3. Disc Golf Towels & Grip Enhancers

Keeping your discs dry is crucial for maintaining control, especially in wet or humid conditions.

- **Microfiber Towels** – Brands like **Dude Disc Golf** and **Whale Sac** provide high-absorbency towels.

- **Grip Enhancers** – **Dirt Bags** and **Birdie Bags** help keep your hands dry for a better grip.

4. Disc Retrievers

If you play near water hazards, a retriever can save you from losing valuable discs. Some of the most effective retrievers include:

- **Golden Retriever** – A compact retriever designed to scoop up discs from the water.

- **Extendable Pole Retriever** – Brands like **Dynamic Discs Retriever** offer telescoping poles that extend to 16+ feet.

5. Putting & Training Aids

Practicing putting at home or on the course is key to improving your game.

- **Portable Baskets** – The **Dynamic Discs Recruit** and **Innova DisCatcher Traveler** are great choices for at-home practice.

- **Throwing Nets** – If you want to work on your drives without needing a full course, **Net Return Nets** provide an easy way to practice indoors or in limited space.

III. Choosing the Right Gear for Your Skill Level

The right gear for you depends on your experience and playing style. Beginners need forgiving discs that are easy to control, while advanced players may prefer high-speed drivers and specialized putters. Here's how to choose the best gear for your level.

1. Beginners

If you're new to the sport, it's best to start with slower-speed, easy-to-control discs. Look for:

- **Putter:** Innova Aviar or Dynamic Discs Judge
- **Midrange:** Discraft Buzzz or Innova Roc3
- **Fairway Driver:** Innova Leopard3 or Latitude 64 River

2. Intermediate Players

As your skills improve, you may want to experiment with more stability and control. Consider:

- **Putter:** MVP Envy or Kastaplast Berg
- **Midrange:** Axiom Hex or Westside Warship
- **Driver:** Innova Thunderbird or Discraft Undertaker

3. Advanced & Competitive Players

For experienced players who want maximum control and distance, these discs are top-tier:

- **Putter:** Discmania P2 or Dynamic Discs Keystone
- **Midrange:** Prodigy M4 or Thought Space Athletics Pathfinder
- **Driver:** Innova Destroyer, Discraft Zeus, or Latitude 64 Ballista Pro

Selecting the right gear enhances both your performance and enjoyment on the course. With so many manufacturers and equipment choices available, it's important to test different discs and accessories to find what suits your style. Investing in high-quality gear tailored to your skill level ensures you stay comfortable, prepared, and ready to take your disc golf game to the next level.

Appendix C: Best Disc Golf Courses in the World

Disc golf is a sport best enjoyed on a beautiful, challenging, and well-designed course. Whether you're seeking picturesque landscapes, technical challenges, or just a fun round with friends, playing on a top-tier course can elevate your game and your experience. This section highlights some of the best disc golf courses worldwide, each offering something unique for players of all skill levels. These courses are known for their design, difficulty, and ability to provide both a challenge and a rewarding experience.

Discover must-play courses that every disc golfer should experience.

I. Must-Play Courses for Every Disc Golf Enthusiast

Here are some of the top courses you should visit at least once, whether you're a seasoned pro or just starting your disc golf journey. Each of these courses has been recognized for its design, beauty, and the excitement it brings to disc golf players:

1. Blue Ribbon Pines - East Bethel, Minnesota, USA - www.blueribbonpines.com

Blue Ribbon Pines is widely regarded as one of the best courses in the world. Known for its mix of open and wooded holes, this course offers a challenging, strategic layout with beautiful surroundings. It's a favorite for competitive tournaments, providing players with a varied and rewarding experience.

2. Maple Hill Disc Golf Course - Leicester, Massachusetts, USA - www.maplehilldg.com

Maple Hill is one of the most popular and challenging courses in the USA, hosting numerous major events including the Disc Golf Pro Tour and PDGA World Championships. The course offers a combination of long open holes and tight, technical wooded sections, making it a complete test of your all-around skills.

3. Järva Disc Golf Park - Stockholm, Sweden - www.jarvadiscgolfpark.se

This course, located in one of Europe's most beautiful cities, is well-maintained and offers a variety of layouts suited to players of all skill levels. Known for its technical design, Järva combines open fairways with wooded sections, making for a diverse and enjoyable playing experience.

4. IDGC (International Disc Golf Center) - Appling, Georgia, USA - www.idgc.com

The IDGC features three world-class courses designed by some of the top names in disc golf. Whether you're playing the "Jim Warner" course or others, you'll encounter wooded technical holes, long-distance throws, and everything in between. It's an incredible location for both casual rounds and serious competitions.

5. Disc Golf Park - Tampere, Finland - www.discgolfpark.com

Tampere is home to some of the best disc golf courses in Europe, offering challenging fairways and scenic lakeside views. The well-designed layouts and diverse course options make it an ideal destination for both beginner and advanced players.

6. Smuggler's Notch - Jeffersonville, Vermont, USA - www.smuggs.com

Nestled in Vermont's mountains, Smuggler's Notch offers stunning views and tough terrain. With a mix of wooded holes and significant elevation changes, it's a challenging course for players looking to test their skills while enjoying breathtaking natural beauty.

7. La Mirada Disc Golf Course - La Mirada, California, USA - www.lamiradadiscgolf.com

La Mirada offers a balanced mix of open and wooded holes, with great weather year-round, making it a popular destination for disc golfers. The course design challenges players with both long and short fairways, perfect for improving shot selection and control.

8. The Beast – Moraine State Park, Pennsylvania, USA - www.thebeastdgc.com

The Beast is known for its long-distance holes, technical fairways, and elevation challenges. It's one of Pennsylvania's most exciting courses, regularly hosting major events. The varied layout tests players' skills, with a mix of open and wooded holes to challenge every aspect of your game.

9. Gausel Disc Golf Course - Stavanger, Norway - www.gauseldgc.com

Gausel, located in beautiful Stavanger, Norway, offers a mix of wooded and open fairways. Known for its challenging terrain and scenic beauty, this course provides an unforgettable experience for players of all skill levels, combining natural surroundings with tough course designs.

10. Rattlesnake Ridge Disc Golf Course - Missoula, Montana, USA - www.rattlesnakedgc.com

Rattlesnake Ridge is a rugged course located in the heart of Montana, surrounded by natural beauty. With tight wooded fairways and significant elevation changes, this course offers both a challenge and an adventure for disc golfers, making it a must-visit for any enthusiast.

~ ~ ~ ~ ~

Whether you're planning a vacation or just looking for new places to play, these courses represent the very best of what disc golf has to offer. From scenic vistas to challenging designs, each course listed here will not only improve your skills but also provide unforgettable experiences. Adding these must-play courses to your disc golf bucket list is the perfect way to experience the sport in new and exciting ways. Ready to hit the road and take your game to the next level? The courses are waiting! 🌐 ✨

Appendix D: Disc Golf Resources & Training Guides

Whether you're looking to improve your skills, stay up-to-date with the latest disc golf news, or find helpful tutorials, the right resources can make a big difference. In this section, we've compiled a list of websites, books, YouTube channels, and apps that offer valuable insights and training to help you advance your game. Whether you're a beginner or an experienced player, these resources will provide the tools you need to keep learning and evolving as a disc golfer.

Improve your skills with expert resources, tutorials, and in-depth training guides.

I. Websites

1. **Disc Golf Pro Tour** - www.dgpt.com
   The official site for the Disc Golf Pro Tour, providing tournament schedules, player profiles, and live scoring. It's an excellent resource for following professional disc golf and staying connected with the community.

2. **PDGA (Professional Disc Golf Association)** - www.pdga.com
   The PDGA is the governing body for the sport of disc golf, offering official rules, rankings, event schedules, and a comprehensive directory of disc golf courses. It's a must-visit for anyone serious about the sport.

3. **UDisc** - www.udisc.com
   UDisc offers a variety of tools, including course maps, a scorecard app, and GPS for disc golfers. It's also a great place to track your progress and find courses near you.

4. **Disc Golf Review** - www.discgolfreview.com
   This site provides in-depth reviews of discs and disc golf gear. You'll find detailed analysis, comparisons, and feedback from

disc golfers around the world, helping you choose the best equipment.

5. **Infinite Discs** - www.infinitediscs.com
A disc golf retailer known for offering a wide variety of discs and accessories. Their site includes reviews, guides, and a great disc search tool to find the perfect disc for your style of play.

~ ~ ~ ~ ~

II. Books

1. **"The Disc Golf Handbook" by Peter T. Kuhl**
This book is a comprehensive guide to understanding disc golf, offering expert advice on everything from basic rules to advanced strategies. It's perfect for beginners and those looking to improve their game.

2. **"Disc Golf: The Complete Guide to the Sport" by James E. S. Rodes**
A great resource for players of all levels, this book dives into disc golf techniques, course strategies, and training methods to enhance your skills and knowledge of the sport.

3. **"The Ultimate Guide to Disc Golf" by Steve West**
This book covers the technical aspects of the game, including how to throw different types of shots and how to manage course strategy. It's an excellent resource for players looking to level up their performance.

~ ~ ~ ~ ~

III. YouTube Channels

1. **JomezPro** - www.youtube.com/user/jomezpro
JomezPro is known for their high-quality, professional disc golf coverage, providing live tournament coverage and insightful commentary. It's a great way to watch the pros play and learn from their strategies.

2. **Disc Golf Guy** - www.youtube.com/user/discgolfguy
A channel dedicated to disc golf tutorials, product reviews, and tournament coverage. Disc Golf Guy provides a wealth of knowledge on how to improve your technique and understanding of the game.

3. **UDisc** - www.youtube.com/c/UDisc
UDisc's channel offers instructional videos, course reviews, and player interviews. It's perfect for players who want to stay updated with disc golf trends and learn new skills.

4. **Team Disc Golf** - www.youtube.com/c/TeamDiscGolf
Team Disc Golf offers instructional content and coverage of various tournaments, with tips for beginners and seasoned players alike. Their tutorials are easy to follow and focused on key techniques to improve your play.

~ ~ ~ ~ ~

IV. Apps

1. **UDisc** - www.udisc.com
The most popular app for disc golfers, UDisc offers features like score tracking, course maps, and live scoring for tournaments. It's a fantastic tool to take your disc golf game to the next level.

2. **PDGA Digital Scorecard** - www.pdga.com
The PDGA's official scorecard app lets you track your scores on the go and even provides live tournament scoring. It's essential for keeping track of your progress and performance in official events.

3. **Disc Golf Course Review (DGCR)** - www.discgolfcoursereview.com
DGCR offers a database of courses with ratings, reviews, and maps. It helps you find disc golf courses near you and provides valuable information from the disc golf community.

4. **Shot Shaper** - www.shotshaper.com
Shot Shaper helps you improve your disc golf form with slow-

motion video capture and detailed analysis of your throws. Perfect for players looking to fine-tune their mechanics.

5. **Throw Tracker** - www.throwtracker.com
   Throw Tracker helps you track your disc golf performance over time. It allows you to log throws, analyze your performance, and track improvements.

~ ~ ~ ~ ~

With the right resources, you can take your disc golf game to new heights. These websites, books, YouTube channels, and apps offer invaluable tools to improve your skills, stay informed, and become a better player. Whether you're practicing on your own or following the pros, the resources available will help you stay motivated and on track to achieve your disc golf goals.

Final Words

Congratulations on finishing *HowExpert Guide to Disc Golf*! You've taken the first step toward mastering the game. But this is only the beginning. With every throw, every round, and every course, you'll unlock new levels of skill, strategy, and enjoyment. What you've learned here is just the foundation—now it's time to put it into action.

Disc golf isn't just a game—it's a pursuit. A pursuit of precision, consistency, and constant improvement. Whether you're seeking to break personal records, crush competition, or simply enjoy a casual round with friends, this book has given you the knowledge to elevate your game. But remember: the real magic happens when you're out on the course, challenging yourself, honing your skills, and most importantly—having fun.

From mastering your throw mechanics to perfecting your putting stroke, the journey to becoming a better disc golfer is never-ending. Each round offers new opportunities to improve, push your limits, and learn from both your successes and mistakes. The challenges you face on the course are just part of what makes this sport so rewarding.

With the right mindset, you'll find yourself enjoying the game more than ever while continuously leveling up.

So, grab your discs, step up to the tee, and take the next step in your journey. Every throw is a chance to get better, every round is an opportunity to grow. Whether you're in it for the thrill of competition or the joy of play, remember that improvement is the goal, but enjoyment is the reward.

Thank you for making *HowExpert Guide to Disc Golf* a part of your game. Your path to mastery is just beginning, and the best disc golf moments are still ahead of you. Get out there, embrace the challenges, and most importantly—enjoy every throw, every course, and every moment of this incredible journey.

The course is yours—now go make your mark.

About HowExpert

HowExpert publishes quick 'how to' guides on all topics from A to Z. Visit HowExpert.com to learn more.

About the Publisher

Byungjoon "BJ" Min (민병준) is an author, publisher, entrepreneur, and the founder of HowExpert. He started off as a once broke convenience store clerk to eventually becoming a fulltime internet marketer and finding his niche in publishing. He is the founder and publisher of HowExpert where the mission is to make a positive impact in the world for all topics from A to Z. Visit BJMin.com and HowExpert.com to learn more. John 14:6

Recommended Resources

- HowExpert.com – How To Guides on All Topics from A to Z.
- HowExpert.com/free – Free HowExpert Email Newsletter.
- HowExpert.com/books – HowExpert Books
- HowExpert.com/courses – HowExpert Courses
- HowExpert.com/clothing – HowExpert Clothing
- HowExpert.com/membership – HowExpert Membership Site
- HowExpert.com/affiliates – HowExpert Affiliate Program
- HowExpert.com/jobs – HowExpert Jobs
- HowExpert.com/writers – Write About Your #1 Passion/Knowledge/Expertise & Become a HowExpert Author.
- HowExpert.com/resources – Additional HowExpert Recommended Resources
- YouTube.com/HowExpert – Subscribe to HowExpert YouTube.
- Instagram.com/HowExpert – Follow HowExpert on Instagram.
- Facebook.com/HowExpert – Follow HowExpert on Facebook.
- TikTok.com/@HowExpert – Follow HowExpert on TikTok.

9 798895 731987